I Am Your Lifeguard

ALSO BY CHARLIE SMITH

Demo

Ginny Gall

Jump Soul: New and Selected Poems

Men in Miami Hotels

Three Delays

Word Comix

Women of America

Heroin and Other Poems

Cheap Ticket to Heaven

Before and After

Chimney Rock

The Palms

Crystal River (Storyville, Crystal River, Tinian)

Indistinguishable from the Darkness

The Lives of the Dead

Shine Hawk

Red Roads

Canaan

I Am Your Lifeguard

NEW AND SELECTED POEMS

Charlie Smith

W. W. NORTON & COMPANY
Independent Publishers Since 1923

Printed in the United States of America
First Edition

For information about permission to reproduce selections from this book, write to Permissions, W. W. Norton & Company, Inc., 500 Fifth Avenue, New York, NY 10110

For information about special discounts for bulk purchases, please contact W. W. Norton Special Sales at specialsales@wwnorton.com or 800-233-4830

Manufacturing by Versa Press
Book design by Chris Welch
Production manager: Daniel Van Ostenbridge

ISBN 978-1-324-11817-6

W. W. Norton & Company, Inc., 500 Fifth Avenue, New York, NY 10110
www.wwnorton.com

W. W. Norton & Company Ltd., 15 Carlisle Street, London W1D 3BS

Authorized EU representative: EAS, Mustamäe tee 50, 10621 Tallinn, Estonia

1 2 3 4 5 6 7 8 9 0

To Daniela Smith and Jill Bialosky

CONTENTS

NEW POEMS

I

II

SELECTED POEMS

from *JUMP SOUL*

from *DEMO*

I Am Your Lifeguard

NEW POEMS

I

Hoots and Howling

eventually you come to.
they hand you a shovel

or a circulating
mechanism that makes a noise like a frightened child.

a voice says this is you
or somebody else like you

and that will do but you better hurry
or the bus will leave you.

you drag yourself
to your fate sick

from the inside out. there's
a scent of rustic

perfume. you get it that nobody's
on top of this episode.

you're looming in the bus window
you're in the city

standing in a little patch of light
in the bar where you used to eat lunch.

you're swimming
in from the submarine.

you're just
knocking around.

of course you knew there was nothing
that would save you.

II

I Am Your Lifeguard

I am your lifeguard, remote
    and mindful, a wind that throws itself from tree to tree

who catches the constellations facing the other way
before they trip

in this prison they call the future
    this mixed, pollinated sea they call a prison

I consider all the apple trees that died during my lifetime

the cheap figurines of Cantinflas
Xs on a calendar in the horse diver's room

    upon the bleached ribs of a goatherd a civilization is founded
the clean t-shirts of the murderer's child they say

under moonlight the towboat comes in
    what world is using my voice to call your name

Making Animal Sounds on the Phone

. . . sit all day in the truck
    rattling off select accounts residual clarifications of pond flora
and gravidities that in west texas
appeal to the senses

    commentaries like running water and shifts in the wind
out on the end of town

    you get it don't you she said this insistence
the way you populate your time
with little stabs in the dark

silent periods
    when you're thinking of local rectitude

tonight they're running
a special
on surrender of the will

    reduced like the day you take in your hands

a silage of the heart's
    monstrosities waits for the news in the big trees
stuffing snow in their pockets

the disputes
    unsettled the provisional government
called back to the ditch
for more training

the one you supposed inviolable

not so sure about things

the rest of us walking around picking up spent shells off the ground.

Dust

I figure the landlord knows
more than he's telling
    about the disappearance around here
of summer,
but you have to go on
without pressing
the question—*I've lost,* he says,
my pretty face—and I
    wear a banana leaf hat in my dream
that includes a spat
with the corner laundryman,
both of us
    misquoting aristotle on prison menus,
and my neighbor taps
almost but
    not quite silently on our mutual wall,
and again I wonder
should I ask her to marry me?
but still after 30 years
we pass
each other silently in the hall
    carrying our tiny baskets of strawberries.

Barrel House

I take back everything I said
    the stammering
approach to the flavored salt giveaway

& my selection
of speeches to the wind

    I take back the rustler lingo I couldn't
let go of
for years

& my attempts to mimic rain
on banana leaves

    I get no solace from the mystery
of life
I said once
I take that back

& my use for years
    of the word *follies* I said maybe a thousand

times plus
my weeping confession
squeezed out after love's last robbery, my

offers of
    reconciliation too late
for your legal team

my hectoring summations
& verbal
looting
    that followed as gravy follows mashed potatoes

I take back my late sobbing
you ignored
    & the mismanaged feasibilities
no one clung to

& the animal noises

& vain
    sanitized admissions
I take them back

    & my queasy insinuations like
a damp breeze

fumbling in the mimosas

    I take back all the speeches I put into the mouths of the stars.

Crash Course

yesterday I saw lowell walking in chinatown
among red foxglove

in a weedy lot, he was turning into a dream

            roughed up and streaming cold black water

from the depths
as I stood in line at jimmy's go bar

for a blue drink to take with me

for the drive out to the lodge
                              it's always timely this

sight of a mansuefied locus returned to say he left his smokes
around here

   somewhere the chieftain playing her twelve string
the sound of a dobro

like a handful of sand scattered across the water

the likelihood of anything happening
is always a mystery says the one drinking falstaff in the backseat

the rubberized underwear is waiting for us all

and there's lowell
picking at his food in a restaurant that folded

not long after the towers fell
        and my sister in law asked why all the restaurants

around here went out of business
and I said grief, sister.

Shorn

the years are gone and still I don't know the disgraced grocer
or the congolese man with beautifully colored suits
on hangers outside his shop, I don't know
the combination to any lock,
or where I dropped my hundred dollar bill,
and I keep forgetting that the hotdog stand I stood in
wolfing a dog with sauerkraut & red onions failed after 50 years
but not before I forgot to learn the proprietor's name,
and I don't know the names of the women
who handled the entrance to our urban garden
where I didn't catch the names of the ragged colorful
flowers poking their noses through the fence, I missed the porter's wedding
and his divorce a few years later that has left
him grieving and still surprised,
and don't ask me about the annual picnic or the trip to atlantic
city, or the winning lottery number, and here's
another summer leaking
like an old boat
soon to founder in the chilly waters of fall,
and my pants are loose on my hips, and where did my eyesight go,
and what is there—what bus or sweetheart—I haven't
waited for at the wrong stop,
still hopeful, as in the open door of the barber shop
my barber, a man with slicked hair and a tender smile, whose name
I've misplaced, says, *next.*

Salt Lick

the smell of dead birds
    accompanies you out to the yard.
the old man who
    spends his nights shouting at himself
comes out on his back
porch and looks studiously your way
but doesn't acknowledge your bow.
sometimes no matter
    what you're still alone. around here the planets hang
there dead as dust.
irrelevant thoughts
    move like wasps on a window screen.
you don't do anything.
sometimes the world
seems easy to pull together
like chess pie.
    nothing unusual shows up for five minutes.
then the craving, the backdated
certainties,
the correctives in a bucket,
    the smell of fresh cement. *Going hell on wheels,*
your ex-wife's letter says, tiny
dots of blood in the margins.

Country Burial

well that was a ball buster
the rank
and despicable

undiscerning
lumpectomy
of the soul a cartoon

pressed into living
action the
looming

circumstance like clouds
that time over jericho
a shift of

prosperity into another
valuation mostly
unprepared for the jerked meat

of holiness
slipping away
like oyster

beds at low tide
into a stink of salt and rankness
the clammy eternity

and elaboration
presented with
the inevitable knockout

reduced
to shale splinters
and unfastened gray teeth.

What Terms

they rifled pages
    and came up with plans for a little casserole
your foster mother used to make

using laundry
detergent and chives

    they said you can clorox those skulls
for us

can't you

in the trees you saw the old specialties
    no longer present at the table,
                                        powder monkey

and pin setter

among them, and heard the soft patter
of eocene horses

    the latest in representations
not meant for use

and sometimes now you prance
and snort

and even squeak like a hay mouse

    and say you are good friends with all living things
but this is not true

Vermont Noir

    nobody really noticed the lantana bee-
balm facetious
wily grasses yarrow
larkspur tough little heart red roses poking
into the wind coleus not really
    giving in maples shredded birches moving in tertiary ways
a canadiana breeze
increasing the daily dosage of icy
means

    a small boy leans into a chest freezer
to touch
frozen dressed ducks
and deer meat
    packed away for sunday dinners each quadrant fulfilling
winter vows
amid the local classified field

    carrion of rose hips and butterfly bush,
shaggy crape flowers
only a memory now time passing in this way
                        unbraided snow loosely scattered
an instigating party
leaving white thumbprints in the creases
of bur oaks and elms
days leaning into the dark
    hearts of eternity sunk in reliquary plots.

Black Shoes

let me off
    at the sigh, the painted-in locus
on no map

wildness chopped up

and thrown in the river

    wainscoting in old houses, drapes stained
and smelling of
shoe polish

the warrior spirit
    a bookmark in the manual of restitution

comfort
like a wad

of milkweed cotton

keys glinting on the sill

grace
    high up in window boxes

the cold facts
the peeled
face of total loss

    pigeon dumplings for supper

everybody
reading a book at the table

the one that
    tells the whole story without getting blood on it.

Parched Peanuts

standard practice
                                        elides like
cloud cover over the port,
    a simple excursion rate enough
to plot a way
forward
    quick change artists
buying up all the avocados, a freakish
system
    moving in
from the west, the new tenant
            calling out the back door to someone in a cat suit,
temp falling,
spiders rotting
            in their webs, a clumsiness of spirit
standing in
            for action, regulars
            all looking up from the bar
at the same time,
the ferry
    operator quoting gandhi, slope style,
love lingering
            like the pink in an old shirt,
fields crusted
                        and dying,
greeters sending signals,
                        but to who about what.

Prima Facie

you're on your way
like a house being moved
across town. *The placidity's off,* she says.
The Traveling Humps, a beggar act,
decides to pack it in.
Planets skip
an orbit now and then,
privation
stalls, players reset the amps,
your particular brand
of love
smells. Still it's okay
to rescind the foment, seek a better
result in Placidio. Sometimes
the roof is lifted away
by giant hands and a grinning
face . . .—does it occur
to you
the evidence
might exonerate the crew,
and a purity of form, a surface
unmarred
by recklessness . . .*—everything*
adds up, the conductor says, *what's*
without shape
and what's not—. . . a reckoning
constantly,
cold as a body packed in salt.

In the Stronghold

. . . breeze taking up the slack,
you get it, the protectorate set aside in a statement read at the funeral

of your barber,
the casement, felt-lined box, lead sheathing, litter muscled

into a stillness we're often after, hayricks arranging their shadows,
shadows of the hills moving in their increase,

the best of us calling for silencers, shots
in the alleys like memories—the light

wobbling like fireflies—
spilled from the bodega, old men clustered around the *jesus es el señor* liquor

store, bits
of juvenal, the funny parts, covering restive stipulations, crowds

astride squares of cardboard, sniffing the bird blood on their fingers,
shrieks, midwives distributing the jolt of breath like peanuts at a ball game,

informal attendees an amenity for the congregation, the reckless
exposed, only figures in the pattern, you can count on that.

Broadside

the small goat butts the chinaberry
tree and stares off into space and you wonder
what a goat
this goat thinks about and what about a cow
broadside chewing its sweet grass
looking away from the herd
as rain moves across the barley field
and you know nothing really lasts
and there is a law of infinite return
but its periodicity is too wide
for us even if we are reincarnated a thousand times
as a hop loader or fritillary
a thousand times each or a tiny silver trout in a mountain
stream or a soldier in the hindu kush
banging the head of a boy against a rock
and the arrangements
don't lend themselves
to much figuration we're stuck
in a fancy passing like a truck filled with watermelons
a girl wearing flour sack underwear
glances up at something inside
saying take me.

Green Waves

The spirit of giving
jostles me on its way to the round-up.

I need
    an inner life, I'm still one who does.
                A life curved
                and shining

like the silver back of a cobia cutting away.

The day expresses its best self
        and falls back. The bindery
is slow,
                but steady. I returned my used backtalk

and wrote off for something new.

It's pretty windy

    on this side of the turnstile. Old masterworks,
promises like jars

of blackberry jelly
                capped with wax, an institute

for acclimatization to the divine will,
                already on the agenda.

    I promise
        I'll go along. I promise I'll crimp

the ends

and stand in the light,
    just as yesterday and the day before.

Text Me a River

first you
fell flat on your face
then your skin erupted in a leopard's
spots
and the eye doctor said
you would have to wear this contraption for a year
maybe two
and your feet while you sleep
curl up like tiny yellow squirrels
and you smell
like a whale fluke
cooked in its own grease
and everybody on the block
says you're next on
the list
and your wife is writing
deliriously happy
letters to
her old boy friends
and yesterday
a stranger
called you by the intimate
nickname unused
since your first
arrest
and a voice you
recognized as your stillborn
twin's
phoned
with his
threadbare accusations

and his
decision to sell
the ukulele collection

sammy I told him
there is no one like me out here.

Werewolf Apollo

. . . cold eyes in the harbor. reticulated
    cumbers, dropped laundry, bluing. a discus
leans
against the broken

bow of Ulysses. the monster
    tires, tips its head back into the rain
like a chicken. All
day we listen to the clanking

    of her heart. Disestablishment.
ragged crows
row west. *heave*
the word for the day. you need

money. or is that love?
get what
    you give, the sign says. arrangements
of hooked-up agrimony,

    puttyroot, green adder's mouth.
doll's eyes haunt me.
supper
served with bitters. yesterday

    only a common thought, slack,
like unkissed lips—
                    the sentient crying into
smoke bludgeoned hands.

Dog Eared Seeds

touching down, dropped by the wind
or birds
leftovers at the grain
market, delicacies,
tapped on the head
by fall,
carried in the pockets of boys, oats,
barley, wheat
spilled from silos in montana
bunchgrass seeds
bluegrass
wild seeds of maple and elm
cotton seeds
sprouted at the end of the row,
tobacco seeds
that feel flat in your palm
hornbeam seeds
black seeds carried a thousand miles
like stories
of love and war
grains of millet and sumac
sunflower seeds ridged
soft
melon seeds dropped by cattle
watermelon seeds
scattered on table tops
all kinds of flower seeds bought in packets
and carried home
to be carefully
raised in window boxes
fragrance

of jasmine and night blooming cereus
shuttered traces
of eternity

My Dillinger

the things he hauled included
dry sponges, a predigested amplitude
or fantasy of same, a criminal record appearing on small
screens in the midwest, a horse hide mask
and reckless loitering,
charges that went back to his youth
in moline,
dreams of clotted rivers,
the casual wave
as an approach to reality,
small fires that got away
from him, dumplings,
fretful singing he was often told to shut up with,
a limp that came
and went depending on his internal weather, internal weather,
the baseless claims
he pressed with varied
lovers, a selection of silky wherewithals,
the deed to the scout hut,
a terrible case of
malarkey willed him by members of his own family,
a desperation
like an ice chest
filled with sprouted roots,
the death songs
of more than 100 species,
shiny fish
scales on an indiana dock,
the taste of kisses like a peeled stick of sugar
cane dipped in a glass of clean water just before he died—

Note from the Night Orderly

Here you might come on yourself, a chef
in a minor institution, or a trumpet player gone
out of style, you might notice yourself at a seaside park,
punching the wind, you might think of yourself
as depleted, jostled by indifferent officials,
you might play at reminders, compare yourself to the frequently
blessed, yet there will come a time
when the development of emergency relations loses momentum,
when on a personal occasion you do not shine.
I wish you would step aside at this moment,
refuse to compare yourself to a prosecutor,
to one who is engaged in a struggle for his rights,
I wish you would sit a while in the grass, experimenting
with a piece of vegetation, I think
it will soon pass, whatever it is,
the day and its henchmen,
the night and its irrepressible spirit,
information about some engagement you didn't recall
will reach you, the absence will prove to be valuable,
there are certain variations,
conspicuous entertainments like brass articles
left on a bench, a summons
coated in pollen, that will sustain you,
bursts of feeling, grandiose rhetorical dawns
and the emptiness will become you, desolation
your inheritance, remarkable to the neighbors,
the ones who burned their houses
for the insurance, to the converted and abused,
who gather around you, indicating with delicate gestures
the vacant lot where your estate used to be.

Ghost Headlines

I keep going on about the trees
or wind or the loose change
of seeds forgotten
    in the body of things that grow, the singular phraseology

I memorized as a child
    that waked me like an exculpate drover,
and I sat in my bed
for hours memorizing *gatsby*

and sheets of printed-out dance steps
like a trail into a supposed
    happiness no one can ever reach while the wind
whispered hair-raising quotations

from leviticus
and a local restaurant menu
    and I stood on the rug swaying and singing
silently in my heart

still laying odds the world
    would carry me in its pocket like a mouse on his way.

Rock Solid

slippery
indecipherable bits
                        squared off. the back-
stage
crew flying flats into the dark.

encomiums
            shrinking
to emplacements
like road

flowers waving at over-sized
                                    cloudwork. the en-
velope addressed to the stars
forgotten

on the counter. crippled
pets
    enshrined in memory like the taste of rubber
in your
mournful dreams.
    the carry-all filled with
recent
shovelings.

capacities met without a claimant
like a smirk kissed
            and tasting of
rain.

Doing Laundry in Key West

I've been doing the laundry
the silver articles the mysterious wide cloth belts
that fasten me in
the undeveloped and spectral
cloaks, the backstabbed shirts still expressing
their show-off shine, pants still swollen
with the winds
of desperation, blank spots from
my father's closet, mother's underwear, the stains
and seepage from plantar warts
bound tightly by colorful
sashes
and other wrappings of old essential
properties, I've carried the big
wicker baskets stuffed
with the gray sheets
of dislocation,
salting
of possibilities and failure
I've pressed the deer hide and the fake
indian beadwork
into the hopper, I sink back into
the shadows of the washateria with my materials
my sortings
and baked-in sprinklings
in my mind I rollick
and stammer
drift in a drip/dry ghostly manner
through the morning, I lean back
in the solitude
of hygienics

loosening my grip, I approach the dryers
with a spiritual
aspect inhale a whiff of
great institutions
shimmering in tropical sunlight,
I pass from one thing to another
the big calderas
and baskets
are my own, the day pelted with
light stands
before me, stacked on my bike, in folded
and illustrated
cleanliness, I set off
down the street,
a messenger of wholesomeness, sanitary, replete—

Dog Paddle

shadows slip sideways, rest
their bodies
against the edges of night like your father
demoted into heartbreaks

by your
mother lost
at sea, and here is how it went
with daddy

who visited marineland looking for clues
and ducked into
wastes of watery deeps
opening

a passage to the throwback of seals
strains of pasteurization
the soiled hankies
of sharks

framed by the multitudes
bathed in a water-
filled grave—
spoke in his sleep

words heretofore unknown in that locale—

I Like to Think I'm Close

Meanwhile I like to recall the stone stairway
from the garden down to the mossy beach in Castine
and who wouldn't. We collected mussels in the creek under the firs.
It gets solid about now. The perspective shifts
but the facts remain. Blue firs, cold salt
black gelatinous sea, Jackie
going mad. It doesn't matter
if we forget, it matters if we care.

Clouds all day yesterday in scrawls, heaps, flat patches and smeared colloidal lumps.
We pedaled to the beach and you took your long swim
as usual. The little gnatcatchers
like manumitted spirits flitted among the pines.
A boy with an expensive camera photographed the birds
and went away. He never looked at the water
streaked green with drifting spiral wrack and glassy. The ocean
that stands in for us and gulps down our bones.

We got out of Kansas City in the rain.
We were eating foot-longs
and drinking Amstel from the bottle. It rained
all the way to San Francisco. We listened to Olivier
read *Anna Karenina*
and you wept so hard when Levin's brother died
that I had to pull over. The sun flashed on the hood of the car
like a wild white substance raving for discovery.

Not Too Far

You can hear people out on the lake talking to themselves,
faking it. West of here they are selling rattled baby ducks
to children. The day is like the expression *get the fuck out of here,*
as close as I can tell. The trees give a cheap shake
to waxy yellow leaves. It's like hot molasses in here
the priest says, pushing his way though the arras.
The one who inherited the outfit dips his hands in ice water.
It helps me think, he says to his mother. The sky belts out
another morning. The rescue squad decides to give up
catered lunches. Wistful probabilities are shoved to the back
of the line. Grace settles like a late edition on the surface
of a life. Something's trying to get through, but not hard enough.

Temple Mount

thrown together vying
for substance and a splash of sunlight
sopping up vellications
    filled with nouns mitered in on noonless sundays

an inessential madcap and baffling
presence the disturbed
    and divagate wiliness spoken of by the bus announcer

some study loose tracts
    picked up off a barbershop floor
others milling on internal islands
polish ordinance,
thrust into

    malverse states, twitching, breaking small figurines
of wittgenstein,
press glabrous lovers
for another round, scratches
slow to heal,

    stacked on a counter postcards of a windswept coast—

Excuses of the Wind

crashed into by
    configuration, puissance, the slights and excuses of the wind,
escape routes stack up,
the previous owner of this collection
of minerals and loose change
incommunicado for years though you sense
the phone ringing
in the next millennium, maybe
less solid than
this one,
    a voice saying you don't have to agree with everything
she says
you can go into the other room—
where in your mind
you hear the river talking its way
out of
trouble, the switch ties,
the boy pressing weights to his chest
    calling for a certitude not offered in this realm,
a character continually
saying thanks,
the bitterness worn to a chokecherry stain,
the voice in the big top
telling his lover
    he's frustrated
and lonely, a body
pulled
from a well, one
who used to all the time
    talk about children capering in a monsoon rain.

Fry Bread

you know how it is to fall
ten stories
and let the wind set you gently down
in a pile of sawdust? who doesn't stand on the back porch
after midnight sobbing
for what's chipped
and indisposed. life's too bulky
and in need of rearranging to give it too much
clout. overspending
can be a problem. and sailboats
tacking up the river
on sunday afternoons. she probably won't
come back.
but nothing else does either.
if it did
you'd wind up capitulating to snowy days
when the squirrels in the park
won't leave their nests. somebody is wailing.
somebody is frying bread
for supper. another's been lonely for years.
she wakes
from a dream of horses
moving slowly down a mountain trail.
rain drips from silver birches.
a yellow fritillary
wobbles into sunlight.
she thinks she ought to leave everything
behind.
like last night's
homely supper, not give it another thought.

Pater Nostra

doughboys of memory,
trench etiquette,
nobody waiting, home, distilled possibilities, the frame
we've settled into, partiality—
stranded—loose—
strayed—
they call it an annie oakley sky,
agents, the foresworn, over-polished tributes
and sometimes you are
so tired,
the climb
laid out like pliocene windfalls, friends crammed
into boxes,
entailed in faltering memory
outward bound,
alarms stuffed into dappled shadow of a camphor tree,
we thought we could worm our way
out
of this like a venice
hangman
night still incorruptible like silence built into a child.

Ponds Frozen All the Way to the Bottom

. . . a self-serving proposition she says—weevils jackanapes stillborn

birds and amputees
checking what's creeping up behind—
a carelessness in the soul you get unloading boxcars

memory not really worth that much she says
something essential isn't reaching us

the tamed strokes of longing just something to talk about

the barber carrying his son to the specialist
in rochester

the day divided between what goes on now and what comes after
the train passing trees
wind-whipped to a frenzy, a stranger in green scrubs—

life only a way of putting things for a while.

Delivery

These delivery bikes, sure,
                    taped-up frames,
the faded kinesis outside delis
and Chinese restaurants—plastic bag-
                              wrapped seats—

like old beaters
out west—Impalas & Skylarks (jack
mormons
on a missionary spree)—you see them (these autos)
                                        boiling across
the high desert, making a smoky left in
Washita

or Orem, something coming,

                    as out here
in the East,

deliverymen on break vigorously
talking or asleep
          on the grass in
                    Washington
Square, bikes
strapped to a sycamore, you
consider
the lemon chicken or fried
          egg sandwiches
lawyers
wait for as they try to convince

a widow
to hand over her pension,

and all day small items
are moving
and children are learning to ride
(with & with-
out protective gear),

while old men in their aged
pickups
deliver instruction manuals
across Los Angeles,
not paying
enough attention, or the right kind,
as they go, you guess,

when later

you see what look like big yellow gulls
sprawled on the Santa Monica
Freeway as
you're speaking
by cell to your ex-husband
who for some
reason this surly twilit July day
is being kind,
at least forbearant,

which you were thinking

about last
    night at the party,
forbearance,
and wondering if it could be a step on the road
                                        to compassion—
maybe, maybe not—or just a

byway, as two boys
on scooters
unhitched saddlebags—you could see them
                                                      through
the plate glass
approach the house, their smooth clean
                                        uncomplicated faces
entering
and about to leave your life,
                          like what,
you thought, apropos nothing—*what*?—and
                                                      what
does any of it have to do w/*you*, and could
even this
    break your heart?

III

By Design

I pick myself up, trot over
to the window that says OPPORTUNITIES.
There I meet Velma in her corduroys.
She hands me a weapon, a love kiss 88.
I blow the heads off a few postulations.
It's time for lunch. We have bent fracas
with jubilation. I carve the meat.
Downstairs—it's afternoon already—
the constabulary is dancing. Officers bend and dip like puppets.
I give a salute to sunlight,
drive to the beach and sit in the car openly weeping.
It's something I like. The sun
drops like a catechism
rolling off a table. I wonder about the night, spangled, chummy night.
It's already late. I find
myself like a handle in the dark. The night applies pressure
to the wound. My memories are all around me
like little songs that used to be popular.
The moon, carrying its notebooks,
wanders through. There's a scramble in the bushes.

IV

Words

. . . let us start again, uncoiffed, irresolute, convicted late at the duplicitous frontier let us say the trees are forthright as usual the angelic spiders swaying in their drafty webs are all right, the dogs are asleep in the laundry room, it's verifiable that as of now the living are still living—or no, there's one gone, no, there's another, aw, forget it—on the prison of earth, not yet completely spent, an ex-recluse (speaking of our time in the womb), a human needing others amid outcrops of felicity and rutilance the accumulations of trabuco and boomer soils seaward bound, we want to express but words fail us or we fail words and can only snort and mumble, collapsing a confession into an inarticulate cry for more applesauce signaling for more space and adherence vis à vis happiness, yet something tells us we have a part in this, like land crabs, and elephants trying the upper foliage, that it's wasteful not to put ourselves into the passageways not to check the illuminated manuscripts and folders because there's something dogged that needs sharing like a blabby ransom note, each of us probably a lifeguard and secretly know it this generalized heart on our sleeve notwithstanding, something gentle that refuses to be suppressed, a comic roaring greetings into empty barrels.

No Clear Purpose

. . . what I put somewhere like a strapped-down body under the outdoor sink
or sewn into a duffel bag or tucked into the space behind the photo of a lover
boy dead from t b the rain in my mind falling on the tiles in tiny waves the
stricken day stricken with sundown almost eliminated gets on with it dusk
on the apalachee and the smell of fish in a river house kitchen trying to sleep
you might not recall the big gates opening for grace moving through to fade
as memory closes down stemwinders a banding ceremony days at the farm
that seem to flatten out as you drive to the store and sit quietly in the truck
as if waiting for the music to start

Himmler

lately himmler's in the shadows,
a long stripe of shade covering half himmler's face and running down
himmler's flabby body to the ground where it buries
itself in the rubble and mess himmler's standing in. nothing particular detains
himmler you can see that but himmler is not an illusionist waiting for a fare
or a man from goa who works in a bakery and is just
getting off and loiters under the painted overhang
thinking about the rivers and hills of his native country and his son
who was killed by a truck as he tagged after his older brother into the street.
it's not hard to say what is on himmler's mind because unlike
us himmler is not filled with doubt and complex imaginings. this
is why himmler is scary, this obverse perfection
like a bomb made of gunpowder, a bucket of nails, and a fuse. half
of himmler's face reveals nothing particularly sinister
but himmler has a reputation around here that's as dark
as a wad of space balled up and painted with eyes and a mouth.
in himmler's hands himmler holds something as soft as a rabbit's fur,
something that makes no sound and doesn't struggle.
the shade and himmler, like those waiting for breath to fail, don't move.
it's clear to himmler that the peculiar advantages of our time mean nothing.

Slops

. . . then I want to turn around and slide down the mountain on my belly getting into the easy way of things the yaupons and the myrtle bushes the voles and arctic hares how they go about things unhampered by blood in your mouth and my testy girlfriend giving up on the whole business the change of gears in the old buick grinding as if they are leveling a rock mountain and the ponds and rivers we knew so well still occasioned in our hearts the flat undisturbed water we sit beside on a dismantling summer evening the lightning bugs coming out waggling their lanterns and tolstoy just getting up from supper to slop the hogs and virginia woolf recalling an evening when from behind the big chair she spied on mother.

Story of the Hero

Story of the hero who made his money by
knocking himself out. A fine novelist

told himself that one. You start off welcome everywhere
and it narrows down. Sometimes you wind up in a small room in Chicago

unraveling bits of string. Calling
to empty buildings and running after the donut truck.

The days interrupt themselves to say nothing's all right.
Yet it's comfortable by the river. At least in your mind.

The water's black all year round.
A man walks by with cotton stuffed in his ears.

A precise comfort.
Tonight, he thinks, I go on patrol.

Too Fine a Point

Time passes like a man moving from hotel to hotel.
The day shades and amplifies, becomes larger
than itself. A convenient listing of events
appears by the bed. There are a few entertainments,
maybe a music performance we'd like to see. Professionals call,
but we're out, walking around the town. There's a canal
like a sharp elbow poking below the skirts of a yellow house,
a few palms against a stucco wall, a soldier changing his uniform
behind the tennis courts. A dizziness appeals at certain times.
We wish for a long stretch in which to do nothing important,
though nothing we've done so far has been that important.
It's easy, we explain, to keep going once you've started,
but then there was the year in Memphis we got lost and
couldn't come up with anything the bosses called necessary,
and the long ago marriage still taunts us late at night,
sometimes after too much brandy, or once in a while
when she calls, and giggles uncontrollably. We're mostly
at peace, unconcerned with politics, careful with the poor,
discrete, well-enough provided for by a grateful government.
We have time now for reading, for lingering asides, wholesome
and repetitive activities proposed by magazines that collect
on a table in the front hall. We watch old women, no older than ourselves,
take on a certain pallor, a hesitation in their step; we see them,
dazed by sunlight, peer at a collapsed shady spot by the garbage cans
as if from that place an answer might come. The day
goes on about its business without much memory,
without the gift of understanding or names. The postcard
praising the new grandchild was returned addressee unknown,
and the loquacious widow in 12-B, who smells of mint,
was found wandering on the beach dragging behind her a mutilated
dog. It's not nearly so hot, or maybe,

caught as we are, almost unawares, by a thought
that seems to carry with it the names of friends
who disappeared a generation ago,
we have reached that state we sought
when we were young, of time passing in cool exultations of oblivion.

Faces Cycling through Unrectified Expressions as They Pass

. . . the upper air impossible to reach on a cold morning like this.
you sit on the curb eating a chocolate croissant,
rustling in a paper sack for something to believe in. your blood
itches, there's a burned place on your back you can't reach.
everyone shuffling their testament looking for the good part.
"you rat faced . . ." is heard more often in the park.
what was it you were about to believe in? whine of circle saws,
bitter dust in a look. proposals gleam like grease.
you once knew what to say, but you don't now. you're early for
the lockup. children wander off carrying their letters
to the police. in your false witness days you already confessed
your crimes. "they keep popping up," you declared, and
pressed your thumbprint to the screen. "you're a dead man,"
says the one behind you, a guy in a derby, but he's just kidding.

Piecemeal

what I grabbed for, a testimonial offered in a language I don't speak,
the tiny ichneumons, cigars resting in brass ashtrays, the duplicates of everything
the sound of propeller airplanes passing on the way to djibouti, something
pretty comfortable about my life if I don't think about it the apparent perfection
of every moment, it's easy to go on running the pile driver or the conveyor,
tipping boxes and canned goods into the bay, time to get going her email says
unsigned unreachable, like stories of travel to countries on no known map,
expressions of joy edged with ash salt water in the bilge the day assuming a
shine like a familiar take on things a breeze filtering memory through the pines.

Roman Songs

. . . excavated red antique bricks matted like pages in the book of stars and waxy sycamore leaves that time in rome we went at it in the ruins of nero's house, the water in the fountains smelled of anise pastilles, you get so the frontier means little, senses grow isolate and frail, doubles lose track, at last it's only the small stations of your puny cross, fields from the rampart like patches of brown flannel, the songs from the doma, "I'm like a muskrat out here," we sing, slant in the face, you can tell, desolation "whips by and is lost," the smoke's getting to me, my lungs the specialist says are blue and I think of the sky in a bag inside me, the unpopular front has lost its way, the probable cause an aside in the dispatches, that time rain washed sand onto the road in a small delta of immaculate whiteness, the split, the vatic qualities I sue for meaning, intensity she says is what those who can't take intimacy go for, the wind in the caelian pines the same wind nero heard the morning he woke up drunk and sat by the window thinking of his mother, the wind slapping itself—"I'm like a ferret out here, a mongoose," we sing, and the same probable cause offers a retraction we barely notice, a casual tip of the hat—all winter we pine in small whispers and sliver-like frets, the days here are shorter in summer than the canal we grew up on, you have something to say go ahead and say it, please, the ramparts, I thought, using my best accent, the donnybrook, the work stoppage . . . the wind nods off . . . one day the earth will stop panting and grow quiet, like a shadow the tide recedes in sand, the breeze, she said, smells of policework, you get so you almost know almost nothing, the day wears its favorite outfit, old men spit tobacco into white china cups, short sales stack up, confusion is only a lingering affection for the best way of saying the man was not really your father, the other day it rained silver light, we saw ourselves for what we were, the actual cause of the blowout was never revealed, a tide chart is included in the proposal we sent with the offer to take everything back—the quick the pit the vitals—I no longer want to be vindictive, the soul's depository is open 24 per, the best of it smells like a geisha, the small sea dead are returned to us whole—*guarda! sei le!*—"I'm like a fox out here," we sing, no other time, only now—

Massey Show Road

. . . everything at my fingertips stained with black ink
or that's my shadow and I don't understand any of it really the shortcuts
prepared with windy oak branches the unusual divertissements like a doxy
batting her lover in the face the bosses converting their triumphs to stories they
tell to doctors in short pants at the gym and this morning I woke to rain
like something poured from a pocket of lushness in the old woods
in those years when mottled thrushes sang all morning and about dusk
the rain let up and we walked out and saw a triple rainbow with one fading foot
and you wrote it down and we were flush with time and didn't even know it
the spaced and rangy bold-faced stock viburnum poking into cracks
and soft tinged amaranthus yellow soldaster raising its young
on the breeze that blew through cracked windows in spring and in my heart
I lifted the shades let sunlight pick its favorites the slack-faced protea
oncidium orchids trying to please limonium and a peachy rose
kept for show under mist as in a cove in the mountains already left behind.

There Ought to Be

. . . the way I see things now, the troubled outlets and raised platforms
of insincerity, the doubling in vision, and the way the g p s keeps
trying to tell me I'm being relocated to a world trackless
with ranges unfamiliar to the satellite, the dumps and carved sulcated spots
without charm scares me, and just yesterday we were trying on new outfits,
walking the fields collecting old shell casings and car parts,
the days still a division between plato and st mark, but now the dumb
clanging of the well buckets, the dogs howling on the next farm over,
speak of a change of mind more elaborate, like a new hireling
trying to eliminate the strange effects that have followed
him all the way from Tennessee, or reports of the drowning
of an ex-trumpeter disgusted with music, on leave from the reserves.

Roma Duro 1

At first even trash piles and the clotted mud on river steps
seemed acts of wizardry, the brown antique lumps like rotted goiters
swelling the sides of modernity you could sink your hands
into, digging for your heart and lemons on the Palatine
untouched by passing years. We received blankets from the Catholic
Relief Fund, and stood just out of traffic waiting for our loneliness to pass,
and spoke kindly to the soldiers patrolling the doors to the Holy See.
You kept getting roughed up by the Caravaggios, especially the one
of Saul become Paul in a blast of light he interpreted as God
criticizing his work, and I criticized yours for Him. We were in solid
with loquats and tiny children kicking goals in Testaccio. The moon,
infected with brown spots and a slow drip of cloudy matter,
followed us into the unrigged coves of the Pamphillia, by the old basilica
and bus repair shop, where we practiced love without holding back, or tried to.

Jupiter

wobbly, nearly excised, sensitive to the undertow of vines
I stake out accelerants, muscle work, little place kickers
and dummy opportunities, checked as I revise myself,
divided properties like a sunny disposition
wrecked by an addiction to solitude, the specialist
kicking linden leaves as he crosses the yard, colors catching
on his surplice, a recklessness, undistinguished,
a device for faking imperishability, I don't know how to
get the trick going, like an assistant to minor players
alluding breathlessly to a compound fracture in the soul,
unhindered, uncourted, standing in a muddy stream
on an idle planet just passing out of sight.

Or Was That Too a Dream

. . . fall not quite a knockout punch, the washateria jockey
shaking out blood-stained sheets in a sluggish breeze,
the desperation in everyone's manner expressed by
a restaurateur shooing diners into the street on rumors
of poison in the beets. dazed, we mill around before
the sunset like escapees from an overturned prison van.

sometimes, mildred says, I believe whatever I'm told.
clouds rise in great lilac funnels into an otherwise clear sky.
we all want to speak without interruption. give the right answer.
no one really wants to skulk silently through empty rooms.

I keep the radio on all day—soak in blasts and
high claims, whipped souls spilling the beans. we mean it
when we say things are tough. like that time she drove
her convertible across the western desert. streaks of color
in chalcedony and rue. not speaking for a thousand miles.

Bears at Twilight

it rained on our mother's coffin, or hailed,
the stones a thin beadwork steadily scattering
as we gave competing eulogies, my brothers and I,
under beach umbrellas, and the hail made the same sound as on the tents
set up on the tundra that time she tried to run away
from her responsibilities and encountered
a bear and threw her arms out wide to encourage it, and in the rain
or hail you could hear the backfires and other small
crucifixions of the city, and my cousin smelled of rancid meat,
and my brother showed me the specks of blood
he coughed into his handkerchief,
and the clouds looked balled up like kant's
version of dynamism compressed into a plausible energy at variance
to will, and she said I want you to stop speaking to me now—

Damascus

. . . brush against full bodies, savor sweat from a thin
australian shoulder on the bus to pancrazio, keen on the lightest touch
like the fading flight of a miracle, the scarred wrist of a girl singing
quietly to herself in line for mass at san sylvestre, catch
on her body the delved hopes in a sparrow-like glance, the careful planning,
the set-asides and usages saved for an emergency,
the revelations that burst at night like distant fireworks
just before rain, the days in a desert town, life raised from improbable means,
dreaming a way through stars like patches of defoliated cotton in the days
when she passed herself off as a child who would come to nothing—

SELECTED POEMS

from *Red Roads*

Dr. Auchincloss Bids Good-Bye to His Wife

There is a jukebox in New Orleans
that plays Beethoven's *Eroica* and it
is toward that jukebox or symphony I am
walking, down a white sidewalk upon which the rain
has begun to cancel
the catalpa leaves, larger than hearts, lime green,
like the ambitious stamps of some Caribbean countries, and,
as I hoped it would, the air smells of decay,
of the river's two-thousand-mile journey
dragging its own corpse, which it will heave
this evening
into the obliterating brown waters
of the Gulf of Mexico. On the corner is a restaurant
where for three dollars they will bring you a plate
heaped high with the obsidian bodies
of crawfish. The crawfish, steamed in bay leaves,
will keep you from starving, though, someone
is always protesting, nothing, *nothing*
really keeps you from starving. There is some
principle of light
flicking across the wedding ring of the banjo player
on the corner, and I would love
to understand this
principle, as I would love to understand
the blonde woman shaking out a quilt
on the red balcony at the end of the street.
I can walk all the way down St. Charles
without speaking to anyone, and it is possible

to be grateful, for the delicacy of passersby,
who do not seem to mind. That symphony
begins with three great notes
like the gates of the ocean
breaking down, but when it is over,
and we are pressing our fingers through the water rings
on the glass-topped table
and craning for the waiter, who has gone to the john,
it will still be Sunday
and the blue evening
will be testing its grip once more
at the heart of our lives.

Liar

What brings me alive
is less than simplicity,
is a company of soldiers in shiny blue jackets
boiling chickens in the shade
by the Erasmus Gate, is the fact that my grandfather
died begging for mercy
in a hotel in Atlanta, and that my grandmother, in 1910,
mourned because her breasts
were small.

I know four men
who paddled the length of the Mississippi
in a dugout they hacked
and burned out of a beech tree. When anyone mentioned rivers
they would look at each other
and their eyes would soften with the memory
of mists and sandbars,
of the grave black brows of river barges.

I come from a country as large as Brazil,
but all I remember
are the wet silver webs
of golden jungle spiders
netted in the cane.

I wake up thinking of my brother,
who, on a July morning in 1954,
killed a boy without meaning to.
And I can tell you that this isn't true,
that my brother didn't,
as he swept back a four iron

on the lawn of our house in Sea Island,
crack the temple of a boy we had only met
the night before. I can say Yes
I am lying again,
about the boy, about Sea Island,
but as you get up to fix another drink
I will tell you a story
about sleeping in a hay barn in Turkey
and of waking in the night, as, one by one,
the farmhands stood out of the rank straw
to greet us.
                I want you to know
that my life is a ritual lie
and that I deserve to be loved
anyway. I want you to smile
when I tell of the purple hyacinths
caught in the gears of the raised bridge
over the Chickopee River, I want you to pretend
you were there.

My sister's hips were two ax handles wide,
she wept that no one would love her,
my sister, who waded among yellow poppies
and wondered if she were really alive—I want you to wish
you had married her,
I want you to say Please, why did she leave me,
Get her back, O my God,
how can I live without her. I'm not even amazed
that I want you to say this. Listen,
I came downstairs this morning
and somebody had filled the house with flowers.

from *Indistinguishable from the Darkness*

The Meaning of Birds

Of the genesis of birds we know nothing,
save the legend they are descended
from reptiles: flying, snap-jawed lizards
that have somehow taken to air. Better the story
that they were crabapple blossoms
or such, blown along by the wind; time after time
finding themselves tossed from perhaps a seaside tree,
floated or lifted over the thin blue lazarine waves
until something in the snatch of color
began to flutter and rise. But what does it matter
anyway how they got up high
in the trees or over the rusty shoulders
of some mountain? There they are,
little figments,
animated—soaring. And if occasionally a tern washes up
greased and stiff, and sometimes a cardinal
or a mockingbird slams against the windshield
and your soul goes *oh God* and shivers
at the quick and unexpected end
to beauty, it is not news that we live in a world
where beauty is unexplainable
and suddenly ruined
and has its own routines. We are often far
from home in a dark town, and our griefs
are difficult to translate into a language
understood by others. We sense the downswing of time
and learn, having come of age, that the reluctant
concessions made in youth

are not sufficient to heat the cold drawn breath
of age. Perhaps temperance
was not enough, foresight or even wisdom
fallacious, not only in conception
but in the thin acts
themselves. So our lives are difficult,
and perhaps unpardonable, and the fey gauds
of youth have, as the old men told us they would,
faded. But still, it is morning again, this day.
In the flowering trees
the birds take up their indifferent, elegant cries.
Look around. Perhaps it isn't too late
to make a fool of yourself again. Perhaps it isn't too late
to flap your arms and cry out, to give
one more cracked rendition of your singular, aspirant song.

from *The Palms*

This Holy Enterprise

The troubled entrepreneurs of evening—
the palm readers, the Mexican bracelet salesmen,
the girl who dances on a sheet of tin—
call out to me, turning for one second
their voices into instruments of love and attention,
promising love and attention, the Grail
of whatever singular prize I have longed for
and now found. I honor them all,
as I honor the priests
and the women who scream at the rain,
as I honor the envelope of bills and silver change
the boss hands me on Saturdays
saying *This is my body.* I have come around
to a pure absolution, gained—like a handful of grain
from the lords—by obedience, so that if I lie
all day Sunday like an effigy of myself,
harmless on the bed,
listening to the rants and vows
rising from the street, it is not because
I consider myself grandee of a greater enterprise,
but a child who listens at the door of his parents' room,
spellbound by the explanations they offer each other
of why the world moves
like a brutish uncle, drunk, through the house.
It is a tone I listen for, an inflection,
the moment when the argument breaks down
because someone can't take it anymore.

The Palms

When the sun went down in L.A. that day I was driving
a rental car east on Sunset Boulevard,
worn down by the endless internal battering,
and looked back to see the vivid capacious burned oceanic light,
the dust in the air that made the light palpable and beautiful
hanging over the pastel city, and saw the crunched little stores
with their brocades of steel locking them up
and the narrow streets springing downhill like madmen
running away; and there was a ridge that blocked the sun,
a scruffy torn wall of yellow earth with a few small houses on top,
widely spaced, disconnected-looking, though down from them
there was a neighborhood of bunched-up shacks
and a street that wound through patches of willow and bougainvillea;
and on the ridge that was sharply defined by the
rotted unmanageable light, there were a few palm trees,
untouched at that moment by breeze so that their tops
hung limply; and they seemed, black against the huge sky
of Los Angeles, like small dark thoughts tethered
at the end of reason's thick ropes, hanging there in gratuitous solitude,
like the thoughts of a man behind a cluttered restaurant counter,
who speaks no English, wearing a hat made of butcher paper,
who slaps and slaps his small daughter, until they both are stunned,
stupid and helpless, overwhelmed by their lives.

Redneck Riviera

We ate at a poor restaurant
that was brightly lit and where the waitress
who was new at the job
tried hard to get our orders right
and brought a piece of streaky fish
that was tough and tasteless while around us
sunburned families from country towns in Alabama
and south Georgia ate the same food
without saying much
to the waitress or each other.
It was such a starry night
and we were such a long way from home,
still so shaky with each other
after the scare of our marriage falling
apart, that I leaned over and kissed
you on the mouth and tasted the lemon
and the dry baked fish
like ashes on the lips of the dead.

Mother at Eighty

You come in dream, Mother, or not at all,
distressed by drugs, scattering quips, complaining
still about the way they torture you. Married late,
you wouldn't leave the party, forced Hawaii
to its knees; I've seen the cascades of your hair,
heard the devilish laugh each suitor ducked, ricocheting
through the rooms; a wastrel girl, uncontrollable.
And press through time to take you in my arms,
to find you now, coldcocked by suffering,
baggage in a train that's plowed its way
into the dark and snowy woods, and stopped.
I see you there, my dreamer, nodding at your window,
unacknowledged, except perhaps by the spotted dog
limping in the snow, that sees you lift your head,
and trembles in your smoky, avid glance.

The Rose

I'm looking everywhere for new ways,
poking, selecting, looking everywhere,
turning the trees over, rummaging among skirts
and stars. I'm so lonely and intense, so
tense and energetic, I'm getting up early
to touch the slick habit of ice on the windowsill,
to touch dust and the dried blue berries of juniper.
I'm shaking and scared of life
and of the absence of life, childless, love
buried out in the prairie far from here
under the shifty grass; I'm watching the white birds
drift up from the south, reading the last lights
in the tall buildings like lines of white type
spelling the future, I'm into everything
haphazardly and wholly, revenant and pilgrim,
I'm looking as I go and I go formally and
rapidly, moving through gales of solitude,
through crowds and the cries of young children;
I'm tasting, I'm smelling everything, I'm
stooping in Chinatown to kiss the boots of
the Buddhists, I'm pressing my bare skin
to the ancient stone designs of artisans lost
to the world; I'm looking everywhere, I'm alert,
I'm open like a child's blue coat as he runs,
I'm ready for bronze and happiness, I'm gamely
adjusting the water level, I'm forgiving it all,
telling it all, hearing it all, I'm ready
for fake silk patches spilling from envelopes,
I'm ready for a "vague splintering of rain,"
ready—I'm looking everywhere—for a delicate

means of transition, I'm stumbling against
beauty and not apologizing, I'm almost naked here,
skinnier than I used to be, almost helpless
or maybe I'm completely helpless as the religious
say is the way to heaven—all right I'm helpless—
I'm swaying on the platform, I'm tenderly
toasting the bread, I'm placing the saucer,
the spoon on the tray, I'm arranging the rose,
I'm pulling the curtain, I'm letting light flood the room.

from *Before and After*

Ruffians

When my father got old, but not too old,
his body went bad, fantastically crumpled,
not like the body of a man who'd spent his life making business,
but like a logger's or a rodeo rider's,
and then only if these men had kept at it,
hacked and rode into their sixties
until the feet, the spine, the heart gave way,
until you found them flat out under a plastic shell,
ripped chest sewn up with stitches thick as the rings
in a child's notebook, until, when the machines had pumped breath
and even life back, you found them propped dizzy in bed
held upright by a brace like a lobster's thorax,
legs shriveled, hair white on every part of the body;
and they never shed a tear, these ruffians,
so even you, the persistent son,
who hated the clink of spurs, the ring of an ax, were moved,
until you could see how hard it was to break a man,
and how sometimes the worst changes nothing,
as if this were a world where knowledge, forbearance,
the whole process of improvement and surrender didn't matter,
and life itself, come in at nightfall from the rainy fields,
stood on the threshold looking at you, without recognition.

There Is No Railroad Named Delight

My great-aunt, a diabetic
and selfish woman, killed herself with fudge.
She'd had enough of being good.
Got up at three, went downstairs,
and poisoned herself with sugar.

I don't think she meant to die. I think
she couldn't wait another minute
for her pleasure in this world.
Selfish yes, but this, a need that drives us
to the grave in fits of passion
and excess, stands for something else.

We're ravenous all right—you see it every day—
and can't refuse the stroke
we step into like a child into a sprinkler's
bristly fan. Inside, for some,
it's dark and cramped all the time.
And nothing in the world of standard means
can air the murky vaults. You know how it starts:
upright in church, it's spring,
a softened, gentle breeze drifts in,
you turn your head, see your child
caught inside a beam of yellow light,
and feel the kick of death.

Anticipation

I think he ought to practice,
but he won't; he ought to get used to things.
It's death, I say; get ready.
But he goes on talking about life.
He liked it here, he had a good time.
You would too, he says, if you'd relax.
I can't, I tell him, this is too much for me.
For me too, he says, but so what. He's not dead yet.
I've lived by pretending what's coming
is already here. I said my wife was gone
months before she left. Anticipation—for me
that was the key. But he goes on eating peaches,
planning for spring, hooking the holes of his life
to the cleats of the future. It won't come,
everyone can see this. Death's
taking over the property. I look up,
and the sky's a huge blueprint
for an estate about to be built,
and I don't know the first thing about hammers
or nails. I roll him to the window
so he can see, but to him the sky is delight,
and the clouds are just puffs and white china dogs.

from *Heroin and Other Poems*

Heroin

I left a message for my editor to send copies of the contracts
to my new agent,
and then I read a passage about how no one talks
about heroin anymore, and the old life came back to me,
it was early yet, I hadn't used heroin for years,
I was one of the few rural junkies in the nation,
one of the few who tended cattle, there I was
nodding on a rock as the cows, stiff with unendurable shyness,
stumbled up to me. My wife and I would eat mashed potatoes
from the pot and lie out on the porch smoking reefer
until it got too dark to see. I bought the drugs
from my friend at the railroad repair depot
just off the main line from Norfolk, Indochinese material,
Long Bin—to Guam—to Fort Ord—to VA—then by Mr. Fixit train to me,
traveling in a nylon medic's bag. I never trusted
the supply—like love—it could dwindle,
or simply give way,
the flexed utensil, like one of those measuring sticks
you unfold and lay across a map; anybody could step on it.
I loved the graciousness of heroin, the way everything externalized
and obvious in the daylight opened its shirt and revealed its soft pale breasts.
The world slept curled in its own foolhardiness.
And my wife came carefully over the blankets to me and seemed
not to mind who I was. We inserted words
into spaces in the rain. For years I remembered the words
and whispered them to myself, half thinking I might
conjure her back into the world. They never caught us.

We missed them on the way to Mexico, to Puebla,
where eventually the line gave out. We slept on a bench outside a church.
It was two days before she died without regaining consciousness,
as I say in the memoir they are paying me so handsomely for.

Real Time

. . . where Hiroshima was, someone said, there's a little star,
and I saw this star, like spit on the sidewalk
. . . and there's a quiet inlet of oaks,
someone said, a brazen light,
and a perpetual return, another promised,
and someone was always having a bad time of it,
grim forecasts and the heart worn down,
punched-in shops on the highway where we bought beer,
and that spring we argued all night,
night after night, and couldn't save the marriage—all that
someone said, will be replaced,
like a city replaced by a meadow
and replaced by a city again—and the little shudder
I got thinking of absent time,
or time without us in it,
and how, sometimes, a friend said, any thought of another
is godlike, is grace, and I read somewhere
about how tired explorers get just before they reach the goal,
about various seaweeds, movies shown in the open air,
about a river pressing in among the trees, and someone said
we all wish to publish manifestos,
and in the decline of summer that year
translations of old ideas appeared like new,
and someone nearly hysterical claimed
he never heard the announcement, and couldn't get out of the way.

Louisiana Purchase

Who knows but that Meriwether Lewis's
lost diaries might turn up yet
packed in a can in some cramped ex-midden
dug up a thousand years from now,
that elegant, exfoliate style
continue on up the Missouri, into sadness
and disrepute, the suicide in a hotel in Tennessee
no more important now than the bundle
of grasses my friend made out in the woods
yesterday and gave to me after a meeting
in which she confessed she's afraid of everything
that's coming. The past I don't mind, she said,
and laughed as if that was something.

The World as Will and Representation

. . . *dissatisfied egotistical state*: Schopenhauer's way of putting things,
thinking about us:
            we are terribly agitated, he says,
no hope for us in good works, or in facts,
    no treehouses or illuminated backyard fetes, no
            investigations carried on under duress
or played-out hunches described in late-night diners
four hours outside Las Vegas,
will do the trick.

Unable to free ourselves from guilt (we're born guilty)
    our only chance an extreme form of asceticism (quietism, button-upism),
lie low in other words, shake off will and desire, no demands.
            Yet, without the framing of a larger hope, a structure
    that sustains and relieves the pressure of humanness, I wonder
how this is possible.

            S okays art (the experience of art
constitutes cessation of the will:
                        beauty wipes the slate clean),
but what about sports or galloping a horse through a field of lupine,
or reading your long-dead unmarried aunt's mail
                                    and speculating about "Roberto,"
wondering why she described the days as "voluminous and without delight,"

or the first time you bought reefer,
            or taking the limousine back from a Yankees game,
stopping off for steaks at Frank's on Little West 12th
and seeing some gorgeous woman
get out of a cab and realizing this is your wife?

what of love?

what of tempestuousness and what of tumult,
what of the irresolution of nights on backporches as love spirals down
all around you,

    the bare times of scorn and vituperation,

the losses, the brief asides in which we fill our minds with the glorious mischances
and duplications of someone else's life, where would
            we be (unquiet, fractious) without
these maddening disagreements, men putting things badly,
women addressing the wrong party, junkyards of rust
and dereliction reminding us of our fallibility, the fallibility itself
and the remorse that push us to do better next time,

and what of desire
almost endless,

    and appetite and loss of control

what of
wayward indiscreet possessiveness under big trees in Miami,
or some such place,
her fingers smelling of Cuban spices,
and the way
she turned to say
    she couldn't go on without a kiss?

The idea, he says, is to remove us from time.

Life, according to S, is suffering
and death is its promised land.

What's left is the inner life, salients
and extended peregrinations and long afternoons muttering of conspiracies,
random phrases circulating among the back precincts of thought,
confused ramblings passing as speculation,
     and speculation itself, the grand moment when
some obscure principle too difficult to repeat or revise begins to make sense, sure,
philosophical systems ground into powder and blown into the eyes of children,

reveries in which we come to understand that true idealism,
               as S says, "is not the empirical,
                        but the transcendental."

 "The world is my representation," he says.

I want to be comforted.

I want to leave the house without worrying about what I left
or left unfinished there.

               Nature, S points out,
accepts us back to its bosom, dead,
without comment.

He means death's not the big deal, we're coming home.

What I mean is I want something to be so true I forget it
and go on fully absorbed out on the dock where the ocean lifts and
falls back sighing.

I notice the gold
streaks on a woman's arm,
the boy boxing under the pines.

Los Dos Rancheros

I can see the moon like a bullet sunk in the clouds' body
and it seems to me the worst has happened. *Nothing*
really touches me, she says, and begins to express her contempt.
For a second everything gets transparent. At my cafe breakfast
I sweat profusely and attempt to comfort
the silverware and consider the water, shimmering
in its glass like precious liquid crystals, to be my friend.
When the government cars go by, the big black-curtained cars
containing dignitaries who will one day beg God to save them,
I get up from my seat and stand on the steps looking at the sky
trying not to think of how what was between us—whatever
you call this corybantic—turned up dead this morning,
but it's no use. Now everything refers to it,
including the young man in the Los Dos Rancheros Restaurant
dreaming Puebla or Ixtlán back into shape, who
jabs one song after another into the jukebox
hard like a man jabbing his finger into the face
of someone impossible to convince, who halfway to his table
stops to throw his head back and laugh with a sound
like a grease fire smothering. I walk out into the
charmlessly evincerating street
where everyone is doing the best he can to keep the dark
from climbing over his back. *Take your hands off me,*
a woman screams and throws herself out of a car.
Even in sleep, the blind newsdealer says, *my life is confusion.*
From here I plot a course that will take me into an area
in which I am respected and praised for leaving her.
You can look me up, she's saying into the phone when I return,
I am the one who fell in love with the captain and lost her honor
not to mention her fortune and now I live

this retired life, that is to say this life of routine
and memory in which I am without hope. Says this
and gives me a look. Quietly the strangulations begin again.
What do you think? That nothing can kill the world, not even love?

Honesty

Maybe Anna won't arrive.
Maybe mordant self-concern will become love.
O you who know things
never change. I imagine
E.A. Poe kissing his child bride, thirteen-year-old girl
her mother standing in for his mother
sweet-tempered raking roast potatoes from the fire,
and shiver with tension and morbidity.
He was appalled by loneliness
by scary apartness, shuddering with resentment
and an alarming sense of smothering.
He lived a while in a bee glade,
high on the island, in NYC.
Anna is
Anna Karenina. Maybe
she won't reach the station.
I used to think the fact my
crazy mother was still alive
meant there was hope. A fool's notion.
She became unreachable
long ago.
In the untidy Southern village I come from
this is not unusual.
People are set.
Vietnam was so great, my friend says,
because folks who would never
get a chance to change their minds, did.
Like my friend's father fat ex-Air Force sergeant
who at last, weeping at the grave,
cried Please God end this, it's no good.
Not the *end this* important, but the *it's no good.*

A change of heart.
Not Vronsky saying okay
I didn't mean it, forget the war,
I love you let's get married raise a family,
but Anna.
It's no good. And Edgar Poe,
this weeping into my hat, tugging the sleeve
of a dead child-woman: It's no good.

Once in my junkie days I kept a cattle herd.
It was winter in the mountains,
prohibitive, rage like a canvas shirt caked in ice,
I pushed hay bales out of a truck.
The cows, fretful women,
their bony hips, moaning, snotty,
when they snuffled up
I'd punch them in the face.
I wanted to punch
my wife
and the side of the mountain
and my life snarled like a deer in a fence.
I was filled with longing
for joyful permanent fixations, and insight,
for play and a secular individualism,
a spiritual life and some unnameable
opportunity like a right I vaguely
remembered and couldn't get purchase on.
It was no good.
It took me years and one mistake
after another to realize this
and even then I simply got washed out,

put aside
I didn't really learn a lesson.
I know it's not so much the mistakes
not the divisions, or cultural impediments,
the threats and isolation techniques
we run on each other
it's the heart.
My father went to his grave unchanged.
So did Poe.
And beautiful Anna Karenina.
And Ovid. Consuela Concepción, too, my piano teacher.
They say in the end
Mussolini was so terrified his mind seized and he couldn't speak.
He sat there swelled-up and bug-eyed. This is not it.
Or anyone drowning or
lurching from the fire shrieking he didn't want this to happen.
There is so much gibberish. And imprecision.
No wonder we lock in.
Like you, I get scared.
I used to go to my friend's house,
sink into the old sofa on his backporch
and read all day. His family
and the ducks and dogs would pass by,
let me be—discreet love—I'd feel safe.
It was just after I stumbled out of my second marriage.
My friend practiced a religion
remarkable in its narrow-mindedness. He inserted
his children into this olla podrida
like a man stuffing leaves into a shoe.
It hurt to see it.
Broken saddle bronc of a beautiful face he had

and his wife a slim twist of blonde girl cunning
and fretful without shame
about anything—I spoke up eventually and got tossed.

I've spent years watching television.
I lie on the couch
eating chocolate and watching television,
arguing with some woman in my head.
Television says the world is not a mysterious place.
Don't worry, it says,
you don't have to change a thing.
And then I remember digging wild leeks,
buying eggs from a crippled old lady
who glanced into the next room sadly
as if a great novelist was dying in there,
and went on
talking, like Kissinger after the war.
And how scary things became when my wife
got up close. Change of heart.
Love leeching the lining away, exposing the pulp.
Stupidity and malice
and a fitful generosity,
shortsightedness and painful posturing,
and things continue just as they are,
nutcases, disputes,
overbearing stupid
claims, modernity hamming it up,
life someone says only a device for entering other realms
—all these in the hopper.
And the tough decisions.
Poe dreaming of a cold finger

picking the lock. Anna stuffing screams back down.
Let go, or stay with it?
The Dalai Lama saying *Sure, sure, I'll take the sprouts,*
including the Chinese in everything.
My girlfriend stunned by the power of her own rage,
nothing she can do about it yet,
rebuking paradise, groping for the cat.

Beautyworks

. . . all kinds of beauty in the world dense pressed-down spots in grass,
crabapples scattered on a white sidewalk let me name them,
shadows draped across yellowing lawns, my wife
standing in a barrel to be photographed pretending to scream
is beautiful, my friend who paints with a table knife
endless solid scenes of light, light on the other side of red warehouses,
light in trees preparing the solution to life, light and misrepresentations of light,
and light behind the garage sale and stumbling down a ditch at dawn
such is beauty, and includes dependable father-and-son collection agencies
and my mother who went crazy trying to clean
everything, and a noncom's sudden refusal, copra plantations
and old bomb holes grown up in snakes and yellow flowers,
a lobbyist weeping over his father's cancer,
disputes that never get settled but go on for generations
as a kind of ethnic memory—Moslems never forgiving Christians
for Jerusalem 1099—beauty's like this,
a lingerer at parties, last to get the taste of love out of its mouth,
a friend locked up for his own good, another
sketching naked men, wrestling with his conscience, consortiums
dispersing into colorful anecdotes, frailty of all kinds as if beauty
were erasable, walks on the beach
pondering the uselessness of existence, the endless variety of the natural world
always on the other side of consciousness, no way . . . this is beauty . . .
to understand a thing about it—

Mute

It's gotten so I can't say what's in my heart
and substitute high-flown brooding
and complex notions concerning the rhythm behind certain actions.
I take walks a couple of times a day,
in early afternoon and later
just before dark and try to pay attention to selected vegetation
and chairs on porches, abandoned board games, and to the attitudes
about life expressed in the postures of husbands and wives
passing, to whatever
else is moving about, to dogs, to the cats this town is filled with.
I am unable to bring myself to speak to anyone,
or perhaps I speak abruptly to a clerk in a store where I buy a cup of coffee
and walk away afraid I have been harsh with him,
which is the greatest sin,
yet I would like to stop someone and say
I have been in love like you
or I think there is a divine expression coming through
all things, no matter how ridiculous they seem,
but I am unable to do this, I simply keep walking.
It may be just after noon when only old men sit outside
because they can't
stand being alone indoors another minute
or it may be dusk when the darkness is like wings being folded
in the gumbo-limbo trees
and whoever I pass is almost unrecognizable to me
as I am to them. I say nothing
and hinder no one. You can hear doves
repeating their stupid cries in the pines.

As for Trees

. . . there are the stupendous oaks and hickories I climbed,
catafalques and monuments, broken-down harassed improvident trees,
unconnected, poorly constructed unsought-after trees, there are bundled sticks,

shaken willows, river birches without footings and over-investigated,
dramatized firs, celibate, virginal pines, capacious elms,
birches divided against themselves, groves come up short, repudiated locusts,

there are maples and obvious sycamores, poplars slender as tax collectors,
duplicated laurels, chinaberry, redwoods without scruples, divisive, whining
    persimmons,
trees of legend and saplings writhing as if on fire,

                                        there are saucy, duplicitous conifers,

everyday live oaks, trees with limbs like thighs, like torsos, like dolphins
rotting on a dock, trees made of deerhide and pleurisy, trees without meaning
beyond the noise they make, there are sumac and buckeye and hawthorn of the rose
    family,

there's mulberry my girlfriend eats of, there is a tree
with no name, there are druidical subversive trees, trees the old man
thinks of when he walks around at night whistling,
                                        there is Sherwood Forest and

delayed reactions taking place under trees,
                                        there is a large following

for some trees, flower and fruit, there are roots poking from the ground,
there is the holly & the effervescent plum, bamboo, lignum vitae, crabapple,
    chokecherry & bay,

there are the trees I have slept under, trees lightning loves, luxurious undulant trees,
immaculate trees and dogwoods forlorn and white-headed in the spring woods,
there are trees in various locales unthought of, trees at the dump and camphor trees

in graveyards & companionable junipers & redbuds & Japanese
    magnolias and crape myrtle
& dahoon, tupelo, viburnum, spruce, catalpa and gum,

there are loquacious trees

and trees that fidget and trees that seem to move around at night,
and voices coming from trees and the famous cedars of Lebanon,

and there are the inveterate hustlers, the trees with red berries and there are
trees like Italian laughter, and unbedded trees, and pepper trees and trees by the ocean
and beeches behind the dunes,

there's rhododendron and laurel, basswood and hop hornbeam

there's yucca and coral tree,

eternal trees and golden trees and trees sewn up tight
and undetectable trees and cautious, dependable trees, and there are fruits
fallen close to the tree and accidents of birth, and trees like hogs run through,

and there is the tree I kissed my first wife under
and the tree she remembered and her red-stained mouth,

there is my friend buried under a myrtle tree, and there's the sand hickory
and the pecan and the raccoon in the loblolly pine, and there are laurel, black haw,
    cherry
and mountain ash and the box elder torn down by hurricane,

there're more trees in the Smokies than anywhere else, there are
trees colossal in their own minds,
sacrificed trees, stumps and root systems upended on ranches,

there is hemlock and silver bell and sparkleberry and peach,
mimosas come to mind, and the obvious silk tree, I saw a tamarack once,
and at the botanical gardens there are banyan trees and baobabs and a cypress

like the cypress
on Christopher Street,

there are locust pods like arched black eyebrows of amazed seigneurs,
and there are the brittle limbs of the London plane tree,

there are simple quivering trees and foxhaven trees and there's a tree
in the middle of my second wife's living room,

there is sassafras, yaupon and pear, there are trees we all love,
cottonwoods and the fragile chestnut, doomed to die, trees that linger
like Spanish perfume,

and there are trees getting things together finally
and trees marshaling their forces and there are trees without hope,
losers and touts down on their luck

and there's an ailanthus behind the
Jesu Christo Es El Señor Liquor Store, a spindly tree, smoke-bit and softened up
by winter, a tree we could go without noticing, and in sooty backyards

there are flowering fruit trees and there's buckthorn and fig, codicils
and allusions to trees and the brief aside once about a tree in the mind,
African and European trees, walnut trees and butternut, hapless trees once human,

there's a rumor about trees and someone mutters like a tree muttering to the wind,

there are corolla, calyx and sepals, red-bit or yellow, white as a sheet falling,

we distinguish various shapes for leaves, the round and the spearlike lance, the
egg-shaped and the frog-footed, the simple leaves of chokecherry and sourwood
droop in
summer, juniper leaves threadlike or stiff & bony, needles blunted,
hugging the ground in winter,

there are leaves euphonious, sighing leaves, whistling, soughing, moaning leaves,
whole boughs moving as if about to exit the earth, rattling of palms,
clatter of magnolias, radiant buckeye leaves as if offering five paths,

there are the meaningless confidential remarks, the questing of pines, forthright
pistachios,
the obstinate oaks, the complicated stirring of the honey locust,
there are catkins and bouquets, single florets dipped in wax,

spatters of scarlet in the white, vague yellow musings, blue silk bits,
rouged lip skin peeled off and crumpled up,
there are

calcified leaves and flowers without distinction and strings of yellow
in late spring, and bunches and unstrung wreaths, stalks of red and yellow,
creamy blistering, there are petals in her hair,

there are acorns and multitudes of purple berries and illiterate pignuts and prickly
filberts,
buckeyes and tufted sycamore balls, various pods, peas of all sizes, tough horned pellets
and sheaths discarded, husks and hulls, burst maple cases
and the shredded dresses of virginal alders,

carelessly tossed aside, coats and leggings, shoes, slippers, scabbards, and smashed violins,
there are the round red berries of the possum haw,

and the splashy, lyric fruits,
I could mention these, epic groves,
fall rattling up its ladders to set fire in the trees.

The Trail

In cities you never visited I sensed your presence.
In bungalow colonies and airport delicatessens

I caught sight of someone
who might have been you, but I couldn't catch up.

I rented apartments and left them vacant in hopes
you might appear, like a vision.

In Utah, a ridgeline seemed to be leading toward you,
but I was wrong.

I tried each highway, driving slowly
so as not to miss you if you'd pulled over to rest.

I descended into coastal cities, often at dawn,
and sat in coffee shops waiting for you.

In hotel rooms
I watched for the phone's blinking light.

I tried to be precise, and maintain confidence,
repeating supportive phrases from my reading,

attempting to stay calm, but often I fell to pieces.
I encountered conscripts and justifiers like myself,

apparitions shouting their news into traffic,
but nothing they told me touched on you.

I eavesdropped on conversations, listening
for the choked-down sobs of the grief-stricken.

Up on the mesa, by a motel pool, I read a story out loud,
a tale in which the author wrote eloquently

of the queerly resolute heroine's
quiet life in a cabin by a meadow,

where the fall, still cordial to its summer,
had begun to streak the poplars faintly gold.

Even then—and I tried hard—
I couldn't picture you.

Zen Do

They are teaching us to stay put, as Mother did
in the oh so long ago when her lips tasted of raspberries.
Gradually the trash fires of metaphysics die out.
Behind each of us, we're told, a bank shelves away.
Beyond this a vastness opens.
Yesterday the woods bled all day.
Conversion of thought into a thin gold wedge
is multiple and serial and endless.
Who advances credit for one whose name is not registered,
whose footprints are his only currency?
I sink into the dew to see what my body will leave behind.
At dawn I go out on the lawn
and shadowbox with the green metal Buddha
who does not notice the world crept like a cat into his arms.

Moon, Moon

The moon follows me street by street—
the same moon with its Camembert and blue face,
blue-eyed moon—or a new moon each street,
one per street—whichever it is
I'm faithful to the one I see, singing "Moon River,"
as I go, walking the streets, faithful to the one
I'm with at the moment I'm with her—I'm with
no one now—I take the moon for a symbol of devotion tonight,
of love's grace, moon over the East River,
Hudson delta, over the Atlantic where hurricane's
despoiling an empty patch of sea, warming up—

tonight there's moonlight in the city, pale effusion
upon the shoulders of drummed-out lovers
and torture victims—upon the priest rolling
up a badminton net,
the child teaching herself to pray—
equal opportunity moon, moon of Puerto Rican gangsters
playing dance tunes before work,
moon of the emotionally demolished and crazy—
impeccable moon—vast and uncluttered, moon
of silent blue seas, moon of Asia and its
outlying dependencies—of the Americas & Europe—
chiseled African moon—it's a rock in night's shoe,
light left on in the closet I enter to
root through love's used-up materials
and scrawled utterances—my pleas for reconsideration—
(moon my companion of demented nights
at the pay phone dialing her number . . .)—witness
to the fulgarious *pecca vis* of love—
strabismic moon, you might say, same moon

as in the stories, distant self-contained wilderness
or astral dumping ground—can't-make-it-
on-its-own moon—like me, accepting all compliments,
stubborn, yet quick to take offense, abashed
and fretful moon, moon white with anger—with fright—
incidental moon, you might say—what's left,
I think, thinking of the moon
as I head south across the city, of love
squeezed in a fist—
call it love—white chunk
of gravel in the nightbird's crop—
only one per customer (moon), yet always available,
the two of us not afraid to show our faces, moon,
neither checking out yet on the other, or on life
(this mainly what I'm thinking about—life,
checking out on it, as if down streets
slanting into a mine,
going down, dear, to explore my
mineral wealth—ha ha—
one who's had enough of trickery and
love snatched from his hands—fix that, moon—)
still here, bobbing up—white apple, head
of a newborn baby, moon shaped like a city—
shining on millionaires recently stripped of their holdings,
on the last customer in Show World, picking the dried
moon fizz from his fingers—egg, imponderable,
bull's-eye—I'm faithful to you tonight, moon,
one more undependable lover
taking a stroll, pretending to walk it off,
headed into the rural districts,
of Central Park, that is, toward the little

homesteads brightened by longing
and flashlights—cracked, moony hearts
sputtering like engines about to fail—

you'll find me stretched out on the grass, dear
singing "Moon Over Charlie,"
supine under my one moon, which is mine & everyone's,
like life, or love—crazed again—
once more—stupefied as a matter of fact,
without negotiable resources or plans,
discommoded and jittery—how I run on—
moon like a fumbled button, doorknob
on a portal I throw myself against—or did—
who would believe me—she wouldn't—
one more time.

Visitation

Fall binds itself, sticks itself loosely in tufts
    and fragments into trees, goes bad in an oak,
drains color down the long sleeve of a catalpa
    like a cut getting worse.
The woman who washes at the water fountain is gone now,
    drifting among the avenues;
her place in the plan is kept for her by certain
    small arrangements made years ago and honored in
relays: same bottles, different men. Now the cross-hatched,
    sugary light smells of the open doors of Chinese restaurants;
a breeze sweeps into the slim upper branches of a maple,
    stirs the leaves to a frenzy, fades, and reappears
twirling on the sidewalk; for a second
    there's no pattern to things, no scheme.
The aged couple feeding pigeons by hand, a vicious pair,
    pause; the old man stares straight ahead,
the woman too, adjusting her clothes;
    whatever they see—a moment ago wasn't there.

Bontemps

Figure you could spend a thousand years
studying one speck of butterfly dust, then go on
to the next and then ten thousand on the water drop the speck
floats in, the ground-up regurgitated
mucilage its accompanying amoeba has just ejected from its excretal sac
taking up another three thousand years of patient
intent scrutiny, and then the germ in the amoeba's innards
another five hundred years, and the refraction of light passing through this,
the fourth wave or conniption of particles from
the right set of rainbowlike protuberances, take this
as your area of expertise, spend ten millenniums
tracing it back to the source which of course is a sumptuous
spangolem in itself and includes the spurt of burning gases just now passing
Jupiter's third moon, one faint wisp of this containing
enough hydrogen to power earth for a million years,
take a grain of this and stand by yourself on Copernicus,
in a dusty hole, scrutinize the periodicity of the four hundredth
atom to the left of the Seal of St. John, and wait
your turn with the five billion others who have
themselves spent eternity doing exactly the same
thing, at a slightly different pace,
to explain this, and while you are waiting
under the one trillion billion stars upon which
the molecules—worlds aspin—all quake, each with its own separate
and sonorous rhythm, each awaiting its turn at the mike,
each impatient, put upon, outraged, desperate
like a man in a dark stairwell fighting off thieves,
and while you are waiting think how one
moment of time is enough in which to understand everything,
one glance at a single tree holding up the rain-shattered light, enough,
and then turn back and start over because you remember a miscalculation

somewhere in the third era to the left of the beginning,
and do this several times, all the time maintaining
your place in line, and then you realize it's been going on like this
for years, like somebody's idea of the good life,
or the way each night the cooks and the busboys gather
on DeLawter's back steps and smoke and tell stories
passing a bottle around, eating crab legs, and summer never ends.

Santa Monica

Someone was writing this incredibly personal poem
and I was reading it over his shoulder
Santa Monica was in the poem
but you could hardly tell
and the devastating loss of integrity
his wife ranting
his cowardice—these were in the poem
and he was sweating as he wrote it
and looking around as if for spies
I am amazed he didn't see me
but sometimes they look right through you
he went on writing his act of contrition
and memory
expressing his extreme embarrassment and sorrow
at how he selfishly used loved ones
lost the money and the house
sat in the car out in the driveway the last morning
and couldn't think where to go
until someone, a cop maybe, suggested
he get something to eat, and then after that he drove
to Kansas. There was a weeping blue cypress in the poem
and at one point he was very accurate about how it feels
when on the street the beloved turns you away.
Sometimes, he wrote, *I stand unnoticed at a counter, waiting.*
At last the woman looks at me and asks what.
It was a struggle, for both of us, to get to the next part.

East End

Framed hard against daylight, against day, plush gray sky slanted west,
we rise, fall down the dune and run at the sea. It's almost calm, snaky under silk,
an army transferring matériel under cover, approaching us. Light picks up
the failed sheen of soaked sand draining. Rock sand, rocks, scoria rubbed
to egg shapes, mottled or striped, some gray, formal, black-suited
dolmen to place on top of a wall you walk by to a funeral—sea rocks.
Up ahead, ponderous clay cliffs, ocher cliffs, broken off, chewed at,
crumbling, stare out to sea. Arches undercut verticals. Each element's
in for the long haul, nothing going anywhere, it's clear; everything repeats itself,
picks up what passes by & uses this, keeps at it. Torn skate purses, crumbled lace of bone,
crab claws, crab shells like tiny tricorns: something awful's happened
under the sea. The dunes rear back, appalled, tumble down and bury themselves
under grass. Something's buried there, that's what it looks like: summer and its dead,
the age sinking deeper. We're following the slink of tideline, watching it run optimistically up
and recede. It goes on rustling, rolling up, the paunchy surf bullying it behind,
orbiculate, unable to repeat itself exactly, unable to conclude, which is the lure.
Sure. One minute to the next nothing's the same, inconclusive, only the invariable
materials, procedure, repetition, the loading docks in continuous operation,
big payloaders, stinking of the Mesozoic, chuffing up, crunching against the ramps,
the enterprise going under lamplight, firelight and sunny day,
combining or sorting out, slipping one thing inside the frame of another,
using what it has, making do, the same ingredients, same elements
always in short supply, the effort hampered by bad weather
and the torpor agitation replaces, by inexactitude and irrepressible revision,
someone dying on his feet, the light beginning to fail, everything
piled against the same limitation, the transaction now surely giving way
like an ocean turning ponderously on its heel, catching itself in the face
with a blow—a wave, salt-streaked, white-streaked—collapsing and rising again.

from *Women of America*

Eastern Forests

I have been walking in the eastern forests
through everglades and hammocks into a mixed deciduous woodland
where hummingbirds and woodpeckers cohabit in the downy hawthorn bushes
and the pepper-and-salt skipper moth, hunted
by the white-eyed vireo and other creatures,
batters its way through broken branches of shortleaf pine
and smooth sumac, a senseless bug without what we call heart,
though as everyone knows some intention, impervious to special pleading,
propels this creature and the eastern black oak acorn weevil,
among thousands of others, across vast reaches of transition, mixed
deciduous and oak-hickory forests, along with wood frogs and flying squirrels,
like love does in our nomenclature, or rumors of gold.

What This Stands For

Plum bushes unable to bear
    the light and the pond that has no place to hide
the reeds saying save me save me are lying

as are the deer imitating lawn ornaments
    and the cherry trees with their little pink
collapsible mouths. The greasy surf,

triplicated and distressed,
    mixed in design, performs
its one trick, lying about it, too,

promoting its complexity,
    which is nothing of the sort. The stupid desire
to find something else with an interior light, some bug

or monkey,
    some planet or lover turning away,
the sexual context of memory

is almost too much
    in this beachy spring with its wet towels
and donuts

gritty with aspirin dust,
    the rabbits like small brown hats
littering the yard.

Here comes that feeling again,
    the emotional ineptitude that abruptly picks up its bed
and walks, that you come on later standing drinks

and roaring, the one that knows
    how to deal with difficult women
and the dark innuendo everyone calls a love life.

Women of America

On the pale morning I left town
I was thinking about women,
and later, in the Rockies where work was scarce,
I thought of women all day
and pretended I was in Florida, for example,
at the little business opportunity my friend Calico
ran in the mall at Perry. By roads in the desert
and among the bean fields in California
I thought of women and
preserved this huge interior life for them
like an estate sheltered from creditors.
It was better, like Dante, to have the woman
out of sight, to spend my time thinking about her,
like Petrarch, like the crippled Leopardi, Keats
and all the rest, to save myself the trouble of real life
and the provincialisms of fact, all that,
the women somewhere maybe in heaven
or upstate New York, doing something
besides thinking of me, I didn't mind,
the conversation went on anyway, its riches sustained me,
the complex multifactors crossing
and intermixing like a high school band
in its difficult formations. Everything else
was simple gesturing, an arm reaching out a car window
to hand someone a sandwich. Of what this came to,
I can't really speak, the women
in their trials and compacts, their anguished disputes
outside small-town jails, of these
I have nothing to say. I was seized by thought,
on a pale morning in Alabama,

distracted as I pumped gasoline, wondering
about Hazel and the grip
she still had on me—How so, Hazel, I thought,
and thus time began to pass, in America.

In July

In July when meat smoke
fills the town,
that's when I think
of you. And June, too,
I thought of you in June.
And in the months before that.
A string of time's divisions, all
of them inky
with little dots where I
thought of you.
Certain places soaked
with you, like the towels they used to
mop up the lemonade.
I thought of you
in the band concert
when the tubas
sank down into their difficult valley.
And later at the reception
where a boy dropped a slice of yellow cake
into the punch.
In July the barbecues begin.
As if it's then the cows reach the market,
meat available.
In China, they say,
men fish with nets in the little streams.
Landlords watch them, waiting
for their money.
If I was there,
an intense person, watching his net
settle onto the current,
I'd think of you, that's obvious.

Shame

I keep referring to you in transition from
one state of being to another like a woman you see
on two or three different buses in the same afternoon.
But this is not shame exactly or anything numinous
and I can't tell you how badly
I want to get high and walk under big complicated trees
and keep talking about you
until you show up. Love goes like this: You forget.
I'm trying not to let this happen, it's a kind of workout
I'm giving myself, high impact, me pounding against
your silence. They all know where you are.
And foolishly I haunt the stockyards and the record stores.

Compared to What

The way certain rogues get to us,
the way, coming into a town,
the tottery chimneys, the creamery,
the boy stumbling as if he understands what it is to be broken,
the way these move us slightly.

• • •

And how on another day
someone takes a room in a hotel and calls a few friends,
and orders a prostitute,
and tells her a story
of paddling a boat among drifting flower gardens,
and the woman, who is not interested, who is thinking of soup
or an envelope waiting at home,
shifts toward the man
lightly touching him, grazing his arm,
without feeling anything for him,
simply doing what she is paid to do, and the man,
who knows this, and doesn't care especially,
is thinking of the flowers drifting in the river, gardenias and roses,
and of a gar, silvery and sharp like a sword, cutting just under the surface.

The way when we hear this we sink down
as if we are entering a small enclosure in our minds
and are suddenly overcome with despair.

And there is another story one remembers
in which a young person
comes into money and becomes prideful

and loses everything and takes a job in a sale barn
wearing a straw hat and making jokes that aren't funny,
and as we listen, a sudden, irrepressible tenderness enters us.

Later there will be stories told in basement rooms,
cold sandwiches on a counter
and a faint chilled laughter from the porch,
and someone who hasn't spoken for a week gets up
and pisses noisily in a can . . .

I was thinking of a woman I loved,
who wouldn't love me.
I thought I would never get past this,
and though it was obvious I would,
that we all do, I began to love the pain
that didn't want to go away, and held on to it.

It touches me how ignorant we are
of many simple effects, the way after my
father stamped through the garden his shoes smelled of flowers.
The way as he badgered us we could smell the wet dirt
and the rotted lilies.

And how later we put our experiences to ourselves
with a certain fastidious pride,
and compel ourselves,
as if we are friends of the court,
to address certain facts that would go otherwise unnoticed,
and how there is a way of explaining these conflictions
to a friend
that makes them seem unimportant.

And the way someone we pass in the street,
an old woman out early
who is too heavy and aches with gout
and favors one grandchild over another and
is slightly desperate and afraid for money—the way
we pass her without caring who she is, and how this
is what it is to be human, no one very close
after all, and how obvious it is—like spring
taking over everything—what we want.

• • •

Soon it is night again and we are wandering around
outside the house thinking things over,
weighing the dark
like a puppy in our hands,
dividing our life into phases,
trying to place one bit of sadness on top of another,
attempting, so we believe, to experience the whole of ourselves,
which has doubled back,
trying to establish representation
with what is already gone,
sure now there was
nothing we could do to save ourselves
and trying not to be scared by this, comparing ourselves
to someone gentled by loss, to a young teacher perhaps,
standing in a darkening classroom
the day of the hurricane, lingering after the children have gone
watching the sky darken and the wind begin to pick at the trees,
a woman who knows something irreplaceable
is dying in her . . .

• • •

understanding how it is possible to place our whole life
succinctly into a frame such as this,
again and again, yet never able
to turn away and leave it there . . .

trying to make something
up that is strong enough to hold us
or move us or keep us.
Like a man in a field walking in the wind
who briefly forgets himself in the smell of lemongrass,
who comes on a red scurry of fur and bone
and stops, convinced an age of unhappiness has arrived.

• • •

Won't you at least, she says, consider
another way of putting things—

and later,
after a good meal, the way we explain we were off our stride,
that is to say impossible to live with . . .

and in the dream, her fiancé's laughter
humiliated us,
the way she wouldn't say where they were going on the honeymoon . . .
for a moment this wasn't a dream . . .

• • •

In Miami the stacked blue waves tumble in.

You can look up a description of the place
in a book in the lobby and then glance up
and see the "coconut palms
and sparkling pool, the Kontiki bar
and wide white sand beach . . ."

Whatever looks straight, she said,
it might look straight, but it eventually curves.
And I said
is that supposed to mean something?
But by then it was too late to come to an understanding.

• • •

The way occasionally we greet the dawn as if we are responsible for it.

Modern Art

Matisse, in a letter
to Henry Clifford, said an artist must identify himself
with the rhythms of nature, make effort,
prepare the soil, get down and grub. Where you end up
won't look like the place you started in.
It won't be that place. I'm obsessed with a woman
and each day I invite the shadow shape—
which obsession is—in the door. Lingerer,
vague disamplitude, you're like rain
in the next county. I sense your presence on the breeze,
smell your body in the damp clay and feculence.

Old Business

for L.W.

A quiet joy appears amid loneliness, doesn't
replace it. We pass the South American men
listening to a radio played softly.
We put faith—in love, old songs, grace
like a gold ring
left by the sink—in what abides;
we put faith in what returns, forget
easily. I read a poem;
it's one the poet wrote just before he died.
There's death in the poem, though I don't believe
he anticipated his own. I think he looked up
from the desk a little shaken
and soothed. But even this, someone says,
is no formula, or even an illustration.
The wish to perceive is itself a mistake, limited,
not one of the aspects. Yet we catch sight
of a pattern disappearing in the mix,
waves from a distance
like comb tracks, claw marks,
the young girl in the foreground
lifting her hands into her dark hair.
An amplitude that closes on itself appeals,
a certain wild hillside ransacked by light.

Talking to Whom

I am like a man
swallowing small fish whole.
Afterward he watches TV,
coughing quietly into his fist.
If I rub my naked belly around
on the floor, where will you be,
in which room, talking on the phone?
It's at moments like these some tragic
element, some quip
or piece of hotel furniture
flies out the window. Little reaper,
Jefe, there was something else
I wanted to say. I've investigated
all this. And stood among the market's
bright fruit weeping openly.
Dearest, they are tearing
down the movie theaters—
blackened areas in which
we clutched each other,
leaving marks.

Each Night I Enter a Terrible Silence

We demonstrated procedures
for each other, taking turns
playing the extraterrestrial. I managed
to corner some affection one night
and gave it to you, a small chunk
you fried up for supper. It took
several glasses to wash it down.
We never could say much
about the future, but insisted on trying.
We thought a lot, but kept it to ourselves.
You were the one passing in the hall
that dark night, a shape like a burglar
I spoke to softly so as not to disturb my wife.

The Night Won't Stop It

We are tired of arguing about who is the most hurt.
Better to toddle off for a little Chinese.
The locust flowers each year like cornmeal in the gutters.
An extraordinary way of putting things, saved up
for the love affair of the century,
gets used by a baker's apprentice talking to his dog.
Investors sink back into the shadows.
Someone with a huge capacity for ambivalence nods off.
The cut-rate sky seems for a moment to throb.
Affairs that began in spring's alarming weather die of heatstroke.
A generous gesture hovers in the back of the mind,
but never steps forward. Cravings appear,
like baskets of fresh linen, in the homes of our friends.
Tenderness is appraised and turned in for theft.
The fragrance of dispatched gardens, like a telegram
from the government, is just a memory. It is so fitful,
so desperate, this business of what matters.
Another's down with a stroke. This way of looking at things
will be forgotten. It was only an experiment.

Dusk at Homer's

The sun withdraws into its twilight years,
into forgetfulness & dreams.
Hard to forget what once we had,
but I'd rather,

rather move on. Ducks in the city,
wildlife in the city, birds:
a list of sightings
tacked to the St. Luke's garden shed: vireos,

a brown thrasher, tanager, shrike.
Who saw those birds?
Some historian, I guess,
someone with time to kill.

Or now we just say things.
I say she loves me & that's what it is,
say Pesco's still alive,
still talking Aquinas as he cooks.

And that fall when a storm
blew all the leaves out of the trees
and the football field on Saturday was ankle deep
in yellow & red tatters,

we scampered in our satin suits
through them.
An old man in the window is reading a book out loud,
maybe, like me,

skipping the bad parts.
A woman nearby's
got a squared-off look. She took
the average of herself and went with that.

I try to remember what
we used to say about things,
how we put it to ourselves.
I don't know, do you?

I've got time on my hands,
it won't wash off.

Old Nobodies Traveling Alone

Like the hand of God

sweeping backward along a passing train,
like a hand
moving down hip-length hair,

say coppery hair, summer in Antwerp,

lindens in bloom
and the architectural students
giving up righteousness for drugs,

around then
when reports burned
under shady circumstances,

then—like the hand of God we said—

all these elements, corsages
floating in the bowl
you dunked your face in,

love all razory
and dulce—the time before

you conformed
to the unfathomable circumstances
of your next position—

just then, the robin said,
before I could really sing,

we were speaking of turncoats,
tableaux,
the formal arrangement

in which the circumstantial lover

alternated with his own dismay,
the two of them—we're part of this—
contingent, fretful, moving steadily

across the space that was left.

The Wilderness

I think of cities that have vanished into time.
I'm sister to the rain. The trees plunge like dolphins
and the city's a ship diving in the sea.
Everything vanished just a moment ago.
I recall my shame at having to watch my father
be humiliated. They made him recant everything he'd said.
And then praise them. My father the poet, who was never strong.

Even in a city, my friend says,
all you have to do is look up to see wilderness. He means the sky,
weather and such. Once he lived in a hogan out in Arizona.
And got caught sexually pestering an Indian schoolgirl and
went to jail for it. Then he moved to New York
and became a fabric designer. He has a shop over on Madison.

Carthage. Nineveh. Chandrapore.
Mostly the important cities didn't disappear.

"We took a boat up the Ganges, but we had to get out;
all the floating corpses made my wife sick. You can
get too much of that in a hurry. We caught a train
and that was much better, though even in the first-class car
we couldn't avoid the smells. India is in the smells,
don't let anyone tell you different."

AND MY SISTERS
ARE NOT WITHOUT THEIR REASONS—for selling out that is.

As a child I thought I'd like to live
on the Côte d'Azur,

which I imagined to be blue-lit, pale and empty,
bare white rocks
and palm trees under a ferocious uncolored sun.
I thought Robinson Crusoe
lived on the Côte d'Azur with his faithful Friday.

And Mother sang in the bath—suicide songs,
Father called them.

• • •

We drank Sanka out on the screened porch
and listened to the owls calling from the empty lot next door.
Grandfather wanted Uncle Peedee to build on that lot,
but he wouldn't. He bought a house down the street
and lived there with his wife, Maude the Electrified Woman.
She was old, Maude, she had hair the color of smoke and twitched.

I am divided against myself, mean sometimes,
but I have decided *I am not a mean person.* My wife
was mean—I said that to the judge. Oh sure, he said,
and snickered. My father's last years
were spent quietly, reading Proust. He'd glance up
from time to time—a look of torment in his face.
You'd wait for that, for the sad, ugly expression
of regret tinged with shame and fury, and we grew
to hate it. We wrote about it in our diaries.
Three sisters and a brother locked into our rooms
scribbling.

• • •

Dear Diary : Today I caught a dose of father's "Look"
and wanted to kill him. Am I crazy?

The Monkey Woman—that's what my sisters
called my wife. They could be cruel, my sisters,
but they had no power. "We live in South Georgia,"
Arlene wrote, "at one with the bugs and the snakes."
Now they never leave the house.

I was small for my age. They say you never get
over something like that, but I think I have.
As an adult I'm a little short,
but not too much. If I was a dwarf I think it
would be worse. "You get a woman to love you,"
my uncle said, "you'll be okay." His squinty wife
Maude peered down at me from her
Electrified distance, head crackling with static.

My grandmother could picture anyone naked.

• • •

And sometimes I think the sunset
hates the darkening houses.

When the robbers made Father take his clothes off
and kneel before them I wished I could have fainted.
I see the vanes of my mother's tragic face

behind the rain, all that,
which I have explained to you in my letter
and would like to spend an evening talking about, if you'd let me.
Please respond to this note posthaste.

from *Word Comix*

I Speak to Fewer People

I have been in touch lately with my inner self,
the fruit picker who lived all those years in a motel.
I shaded my story so it proved everything I did was
by intention. After each love affair, each participant
received a little gift. I mean someone always said:
You didn't really love her. I speak to fewer people
than ever. No matter what it looks like—I say this
every chance I get—something divine is going on.
And wonder: Is it? I'd like to lose a little weight.
Just the same, the marriage had its good points.
I still can't tell you what I am known for. I'm easily
shamed. On my walks I hope to meet someone interesting,
someone I have been headed toward all my life,
or simply someone without too much guile, a friendly
person with a little intelligence. Maybe we will
walk along together, talking about romance or trucks.

Evasive Action

. . . the clipped possessive moment, the barber on his porch
cutting his son's hair, who looks for a second straight into the sun
and then back at his son's head now a golden, nodulous remnant,
a flower if he likes or Lenin's bumpy skull, he puts his scissors down
and goes inside and apologizes to his wife, who doesn't understand,
but who accepts his words like a private harvest she's storing up,
and then the son, who's going into the army, comes in, half cut,
and sees them and thinks he understands years of bickering,
but doesn't, and goes on to the battlefield where he writes his sister
saying we are not far from the truth of things, watching beyond his hand
two scorpions pick at each other, and thinks of days by the river, of his
father recovering from cancer, singing a song his grandmother memorized in Vienna
and his father, who hated his own mother, cursing her, revoking the song,
and the next moment he's blown apart and then sent home in a metal coffin
and the parents and the sister get up early on the day of his funeral
and eat breakfast silently on the porch, and this is going on barber after barber.

Abuses in the Big Hotels

Small birds, damaged by shellfire, slant against the light.
"The descent of wisdom . . ." the dictator begins,
and pauses, recalling his mother's wine-reddened face.
A residue of depression become ill will, a sensation
of engorgement, and an undeveloped moment in which the spirit stalls,
falls back and drops to its knees nervously trembling,
swing by. The old Cuban woman in the artist's photographs
seems less sinister today. Not long after midnight
sounds near the library like gunshots. The public yearns
for happiness, for exhilaration, instruction and seamless joy.
A frame-up fails. Light pours imprecisely over white coffins
tipped on their sides. An officer taking apart a man's face
regrets his lack of schooling. Acquaintances, called by the police,
resentfully clean the victim's apartment. A child is helplessly considerate,
misses what was said, wanders out of the backyard and disappears.
Grace naps in an empty garage. An illusion,
mistook for happiness, fades one afternoon about four.
The old man they watched six years straight do nothing yet
died between shifts. He left a bloody shirt once, in Tenerife,
and never went back for it. "I loved," the dictator says,
"the way my mother's body moved when she strolled along
holding herself in her arms. I have always loved
the elegant sway, the curve like infinity's cul de sac,
the seductive and unappeasable . . ." and stops talking.

Evergreens

The year I admitted I was lonely
I didn't know what I was saying
    I said the nights are rough here
they have minikins & clowns
old postulates
taking out the trash and you
    get lonely sometimes. I didn't know
how one thing leads to another
like a smell under the house
    and then you're talking about the payoff
when you don't even want to
you want them to listen
like people with taps on their shoes
    who later as they heavily, roguishly dance,
think well of you.

Hollyhocks

. . . rosettes, or like those figs packed in a wheel:
hollyhock blooms stripped back to seed cases, summerworn capsules like tires
racked at a Gulf station in the dusty West of movies,
            the stems of these flowers known in roadside
Navajo gardens rubbed raw, frayed, strips of pale plant matter
hanging from them like Brian Donlevy's

collar shreds
(in *The Glass Key*)
as he dresses to do the worst
to get the best (time
    stuttering, smirking
its way out of the area, slithering), the stringy bits of coating

stripped from the peduncle,
            the tall skinny (stringbean) hollyhocks, and the
blooms *not like*
collar parts, or maybe studs (a spiky inflorescence),
rosaceous,
and Donlevy, like all of us,

secretly a hero, rugged
and noisy,
    filled with the lively force and animal good spirits
(Alan Ladd
his great fixer says, *He's on the dead up & up*)
            not always sufficient—I guess—

to keep us alive long enough
to bloom & proliferate, but must perish—we've agreed—

so it's not even a race, but only
a flowering, that fades—*one*
  after the other—leaving seed satchels,
wreaths, discs, coronals, festoons, chaplets & annulations,
not raiment, a springboard or destiny, but like those columnar starter lights
at drag races, flashing on in June,

            signaling summer's all clear,
the flowers tissuey yet slightly reptilian, *sostenuto,*
not spiraling, but set at intervals along the spike that's tough
and straight, the whole
shebang a fresh seeding
like a broken marriage you get up out of

and build a new life from, the attempt
to stay clear of what nearly killed you,
        like one gazing
at a dusty desert landscape
             who sees hollyhocks
blooming in the old woman's garden

next door—signals they look like—the garden tipped,
spun around like someone hit by a car
thrown down busted in a ditch
  and left there, torn, little brilliant lights
and important points of elegance & forthrightness
done in, flowers

like the shed skins of small gods or Bikini Atoll
shambling back,
  those bushes

with their internal gizmos and genetic structures rattled
dazed and pummeled near to shit,
                    maimed, little

Krazimotos, Igors, Ratzos
      and amiable mental midgets putting
forth a curtailed, counter radiance (like everybody), freakish,

like Alan
Ladd (imagination
& delicacy around the mouth, his
inability to miss
      what's really going on) revivifying
after William Bendix

beats his soul nearly out of his body,
the frayed
      and dying hollyhocks,
and the whole upended affair—
pattern scrambled—including the old lady's nondescript dog,
that, slowly,

like an aged *fabricateur* forgetting where he is,
                              or not caring anymore,
Samuel Beckett (*por ejemplo*) in the nursing
home
glancing up from a last piece of work,
starting to forget

      the intolerable situation—turns his big head, the dog,
among the broken stems of great flowers—kings,

queens
mit regalia—
garden worn to the nap,
    the underdebris, (shredded, dry) like a bed now—
turns his head and—unable
to comprehend the works of humankind—looks at you (so you say—*we say we say*),
    tenderly.

Like Odysseus, Like Achilles

Homer sleeping on the ground,
little rock angle if he's lucky, goatskin
tarp, he's headed to some nobleman's

house for Thanksgiving, it's late in the season,
Homer's wondering
why at his age he's still thinking of women, doxies

he calls them, heartless charmers, he wants
to get up and pace,
but the boy's fast asleep, and truth is,

he knows it's not the girls,
it's him, his craving, these broads,
he can't shake the habit, the loneliness

and the harsh poetry of life are simply too much
w/out chicks in it, the disconsolation, you
name it: troglodytic personal ghettoism,

godforsaken secludinous isolato apartheid,
Maraboutian pillarist enmonkment & eremitistic adytum,
he could go on and on, but he never does,

he's just a country boy, simple and straightforward,
his heart like a used-up farmer
in a bad crop year, longing for a life at sea.

Little Swan Songs Being Sung All Down the Block

Consider the good-byes you'd say to a baby in a satchel (*I got*
to get going now) the firebreaks broken through just in time
and the snarling child overrun by shame the unrestrictible
beauty of whole countries. Consider the rapidity
with which the world gets back to us the remarkably
festive nature of bridges in general. Consider how pigeon shadows
like black tears fall down the side of the Hotel W as you
grow more distant from possibility that is to say
are still on the killer's list. Consider please the
disputes settled by a glance the runaround still possible
mostly rescinded. Consider the refusal to let you in
the blasted heaths of love postmortems taking place in parking lots
and the rear projections of those—by themselves—falsely accused.
Consider the established way of speaking the unverifiable
particularities alluded to by a series of contestable affidavits
and a spiffy gent just cutting his eyes away. Consider
how dear the old man's look just was the subtlety uncapturable really
except if then in the royal flush of words if you were there to see it
the (consider this) still upright
moment beckoning like a tempestuous new lover just starting the tally.

Illustrated Guide to Familiar American Trees

I don't get it about the natural world.
Like, greenery,
without people in it, is supposed to do what?

City sunlight, I say, how can you beat it—
the walk to the pool after work, shine
caught in the shopkeeper's visor, bursts.

I see myself moving around New York,
snapping my fingers, eating fries.

My ex-wife's out in California.

I wish she was over on Bank Street,
up on the second floor,
and I was on the way there
to call to her from the sidewalk.

There's a cypress on that block, two honey
locusts and an oak. I love those trees
like my own brothers.

Out of the Way Bungalow-Style Areas

Sometimes love's vagrancy (whatever you call it)
overwhelms all but the most robust subscribers
and dishonest as it may sound the whole cramped enterprise
is given only a few minutes to clear out of town.

We were touchy that year, all year,
at least until the old lady died. Perhaps a singularity
enraptured you, caused the sell-off
and the false positive. Compare your notes

with the sample addresses, the ones
the boss started to give, but then just couldn't.
Outside the metropolis
you hardly find any restaurants worth eating in. Yet

the places are always full. Little families, conversation groups,
a sense of the fell and distracted nature of humankind,
the displaced circular reasoning one gets into after a gambling loss,
these show up, disperse among the tables

and fade into the background.
It appears we'll be here just long enough. For whatever
the thing is that knows no human reason to have its say. Or something
other, she explained, and passed the biscuits around.

Lariats

I suppose I want forgiveness for lying so bluntly
and not getting around behind the house
where the real work is, and I guess
I never got used to the suppositions
and colorful descriptions of harmonious doings
at the cotton gin or ancient château become a famous hotel.

The designs I had of random placement, of particular amenities,
passed with the night. I go where the fruit cups are.

Now the descriptions I read in the paper
of souls caught thieving, caught lying
about the body, always fit, always ring true.

I bought a car in Alabama
and drove it to Texas, traded it for a horse
and crossed into Mexico where I got arrested and sent back in a van
to Brownsville, put in a dormitory-style jail
and, after roughing up by agencies unleavened by courtesy, got out
on a hot dawn and sat in a cafe eating hominy soup,
thinking of Kafka and Henry Miller who
in his great books never mentioned visiting churches or the Louvre,
and wondered how my horse was, an ignoble, bitter animal I disliked.

Oh Yeah

Afterward my friend explains
how awkward it is for him when there's no set procedure
and like a country maddened by grief
where the populace runs shrieking into the jungle
he is forced to make conversation
with some man he has no control of, like the time in New Orleans
when his wife rolled the Mercedes and showed up
with half her hair burned off cursing the police,
or he was just standing there, he said, like a god, *Christ*
you should've seen me, and this nut started talking about
his farm in Mexico, and suddenly my friend sensed
no one knew anything, really, about how to keep loving
anyone, anyone at all,
and that's how you get off on these little fishing trips
where you lie in the tent by yourself reading
the journals of lost explorers, and without looking
you can sense the sun, the spectacular evaporate,
erasing everything, that's how you take it, personally,
as if a secret shelter is slowly being exposed to scrutiny
or the joke's starting to make sense.

Meaty Chunks

If I ask forgiveness will the sweetgum tree
bend down to me, or cherries fall in my lap,
or the substitute driver,
the one who never liked us, will he honk compunctiously—
a man troubled in sleep by furious agents
of change—become like us
in a knowledgeable way? Will I become the one
who on the group campout makes potato pancakes
and later walks by the lake fretting about Mother,
dying of a tumor in Portland? *Where to?* ask
the oversubscribed,
turning for direction to self-published maps
scribbled over with rage.
The pride I thought so much of
has, if not abated, turned into a sleeping pill.
I gain through decrease,
like a goalie. And sit in my car eating raspberry glacé,
waiting for the singalong to begin. The top of something
wants to come off, but still
I back away, like a trainee before a bear with its head
in a bucket. Ludicrous, I think, sweating
and scared, ordered to continue with whatever it was I just forgot.

Leaves in the Subway

Breeze stirred by a train's
arrival lifts a green, yellow and pale red maple leaf,
spins and tosses it onto a bench where a woman in
dark blue like an old-fashioned governess moves down a bit to give it room.

The subtlety of forgiveness is more important and the twice-told
matter of a young girl's triumph in her software class,
stays with us longer, I suppose, and then we have the carefully
placed moments in which one who has made trouble all along,
in an unfashionable flourish
and a prank conceived out of a need to quell loneliness,
attempts to catch the attention of those in the know, and fails.

I've given religion much thought and now sometimes attend services.
I don't suppose it'll hurt, unless I meet
a malefic individual who gains influence and makes me
do illegal things. But this probably won't happen. I got caught
a few years ago in an internet scam, and
spent several months
retrieving my identity, but for a while now
I've been untouched by crime. The days mount like saucers on a table.
I give to charity when I think of it and try not to dwell
on where the money really goes; being kind is the idea, after all.

Yesterday I drove to the mall and walked around.
The young pear trees were just transferring their business to fall.
They looked nifty and neat, not too tall and free of messy fruit.
I thought of Stendhal in his late years, still working,
without much success, and of Follain and his penetrating
sight, young girls climbing French hills
to their big or little deaths, never having

indicated much or spoken. My wife and I are planning
a move to France. It'll be fun. Next week we'll visit the embassy
to chat about expectations and services. Out my window fall's
piecing things together, sweeping up
and generally preparing the park for winter. Soon we'll be sledding
on the white Paris hills. I have a new snowsuit and boots
and can't wait to try them out. It's another way of making friends.

Extremadura

I'm tired, spent really,
but don't say much, lean toward the rookeries, spirulina
days, effect trooperish refrains, undeliquent and pressed,
not hardy but persistent still, in a fading way,
feel dunked-on, put-upon, dry-hearted often
in face of grief, bear trouble poorly, issue bulletins
to the Dept of the Interior
requesting stays and clarifications, sent to former
addresses. Querulous, taking too long to pee,
drafty, windy I mean, poised, or stuck, interested
in repellents,
chromium cures, provisional governments that stay on
forgetfully, crudely demanding
and ineffectual in a familiar way. Partial caps, vein splices,
unilateralisms, useful tips. Enormity
breaks through. The striation, evisceration of sunrise, dampened yellows
and parlous, disintegrating reds,
speedy particles stream, gravity, unspent grief, quivers at the fascia,
life a nolo contendere thing,
distent, then deflated, gurgling; raw winter fields,
boys kicking a football, a grainy, bottom-heavy mist almost too much
to bear, numb arguments pressed locally and taken
for universal truths, the next geezer over complaining,
or was that me, pushing at the fence that sags with our weight, and holds.

Pied Noir

At four I was put into steel-ribbed jackboots
in an attempt to shore up my ankles that they
said were too weak to hold me up on their own,
implausible, incomplete, half-wit mélanges,
frappés of bone and sinew, strapped into the
heavy oil-reeking burrow-like ordinance of my
black storm trooper boots that took twenty
minutes and all my tottish gifts to lace
up. I already knew how to read, having taught
myself by religiously studying the *Pogo* comic
books (Walt Kelly, artist) and so I knew from
the instructions, purpose and disclaimers
that accompanied the boots that these infernal
contraptions were designed to put the afflicted
child on equal footing with his peers. Equal
footing! Only if other children's feet were
set in cement. At once I knew that these clod
stompers were only another contrivance
conjured by my father to facilitate his task
of getting rid of me. Maybe he thought wearing
them would drive me to suicide—a laughingstock,
a humiliated person—or cause me to stumble
into traffic or provoke bullies to the point
that they would beat my head in with my
own steel-capped shoes. Nearly weeping,
grimacing with shame and unable entirely to
suppress his derisive laughter, Pop watched
with pornographic glee in his eyes as I laced
the leather pachyderms up. My choked-down
tears stung in my throat like Red Devil hot
sauce. In the backyard my mother shrieked

negatively, spewing her addled jazz. The
truth was I believed them. I accepted that
I was deformed, a local mutant who couldn't
walk straight or well. As I had raced barefoot
across lawns or dangled my feet in the
runoff creek I felt no pain or awkwardness.
But something must be wrong; they said so—
something invisible, something powerful
like the work of God, and it had warped
my toes and bent my ankles and stripped my
metatarsals of their power. At the same
time something else, a trashy, renegade
voice, only a tendency, a leniency, a notion,
rose in me. It rejected all of the above
and suggested I was in the hands of killers.

The Greeks

I've been depressed lately about my general lack of advancement,
maybe that's it, nothing's coming out right,
and I thought man this is like a Greek tragedy,
but I read a book that said such business wasn't even ironic
and in most cases expected. I dream sometimes of going away,
but not as often as I used to, I've already cut out
so many times, started over, I don't know where I'd go
or don't trust—something, I stay where I am.
At the coffee bar where I go at daylight to work things through
a woman in straitlaced clothes comes in and goes out
nervously, asks for coffee, picks at her cuticles as she waits
looking around—I notice this
but it's as far as I go, the rounded cheeks, flat black eyes,
yes they're in there too, but no further than this, I don't speculate
for example about what she's doing. I'm growing more numb as time
passes except for the moment when the person next to me is spoken to
and I become acutely embarrassed, like an adolescent who's sure
everyone can see through to his mucky shame. I see many others
who're weary and nervous and sore of heart,
but you can't speak to them in a city like this
without taking a chance on getting battered. Best to save
your tender feelings for the totally bamboozled, the foot-dragging
crumpled homeless guy who pulls himself hand over hand through the subway car
bleating and holding out his wrinkled paper cup. He's like us, metaphorically,
a man with work to do, getting on with it, some slaphappy liberator
God's taken up on the mountain and beat the shit out of
and sent back down sans a tablet of laws or any instructions whatsoever.
Now he's here, dopey and persistent, we know the story, we're part of it,
a bunch of Greeks the gods have turned their faces from,
we're down here on the grimy beach arguing and ruining everything,
getting up each day like men getting out of garbage bags behind the 7-Eleven,

hoping some beauty's beckoning, some version, unstable but plucky,
something safe and new, might show up. By now I've encountered
a thousand ways of looking at life, read books about it,
yet still I like to venture out at dawn
which even as it begins is ending, gray streets slumped
in fog. Sometimes I catch sight of a fresh compilation.
It's a variable, meaning. Then I notice in her old driver's license photo
the sadness in my ex-wife's face; it was there all the time.
She's out of the picture now, you might say,
off plumbing the atrabilious instant out in L.A. I remember waking up
after midnight thinking she's such a Nazi about the damn covers.
Wanting out, going into the bathroom to argue with myself,
nearly stupefied with regret that I'd ever married her.
Yet when it ended I cried for months. Is this Greek?
I don't know, human maybe. Everything's more tangled than ever.
Just now I'm thinking of old drunks, how their faces look doubled in size,
or the head shrunk, the skull back of the eyes,
brows tufty and separated by deep lines,
mouth slightly agape, lips slathered with a
purpose that's nearly faded out, the space between them shadowy
as if they've taken a small bite out of the dark
and hold it in their mouths, waiting for a drink to wash it down.
I'm minutes away from something important,
yet I don't know if I'll recognize it when it gets here.
Philoctetes, somebody, I think of him,
the wound that never heals, *there's* a story I could go for,
the slow stump up the beach towards the truth, or
maybe only the facts, some horrible revelation only minutes away.
Maybe stop for a donut or something, Phil, notice the pattern
if you can call it that, the windy momentum in the trees.

Clean

Flattened, sprawled out, snuffling like a dog,
I sniff the expectorate and the feculent lost phenomena,
the shavings and culls, the drifted apart discards
and answers become complications heaved into the grass.
I slide on my belly over the damp places
where old men lay down to try the earth on for size.
In misused areaways behind buildings, among the grassy footings
and slippery spots where disgusting practices ended up, I find
a kind of happiness. My body's covered with what's down there.
Mottled and stained, I've become one with the particulate, the crumb,
the soiled and ineradicable section, the sulcated and unattended spot.
I follow the hog trail of longing. The lowdown is my fortune.
The fundament, the footing, the radicle, the rhizoid, the parquet.
Mouth stuffed with dirt, I chew the bulletins of governance and desire
and take comfort in the filth, in the place
of failure and exudation. I am at home among fistulas
and burned patches, down there with the stems, the shrieks that failed
to arouse pity, the exogenous hopes tossed out with the trash.
What I gather about me was there before I came.
It is often slick and pulpy like a mango,
hot like the scrap of cat hide the sun shines on,
and in its capacity to represent the likelihood of a life beyond
integrity and consummation, I am solaced.
I make small flapping motions, I scurry
my feet and spirate, dragging myself forward,
paying a manifest attention to the tiny voices of ant wings and drying spittle,
and I repeat what they say. In the faint resettlings
of dust and endlessly reducible fractions
I recognize my own voice. Like them I am not saying anything important.
Like them—like the torn-off bee abdomens and locust petals,
the crusts—I have left behind the designs

and purposes I was built for. I am free to inch along,
without meaning. Among the lost
I'm found. I present to myself the unoccupied remainders and
disarranged failed circumstances, the painted tin receptacles
and scuffed flooring of transience: among the discarded, discarded:
among the deserted, the marooned, the forsook, I am part of things.
Now the casual elimination is acceptable to me,
the object hurled down in fury or bitterly tossed aside,
the letter torn to pieces,
the wedding ring in feckless ceremony placed
between two slightly larger stones and covered with moss,
the torn away excess
and deliveries that failed to reach their destinations—
all are acceptable, as are the messy discharges and the exuviation.
Relinquishments, the scattering of pieces, erasures and jettisons,
the fatally incomplete, are equal in my sight.
I flutter and scramble, I drag myself overhand,
leaving a trail, abreast of the trash,
keeping up with dereliction, equal with the failed repairs,
the designs growing more marginal as we speak.
It is here I find the endings that in their perfections of absolute loss
have become beginnings again, the bitten-off phrases and
inconspicuous wadding of spoiled opportunity about to start over.
I see the lost revamped. The mortified recast.
The crapped out recombined with the useless to make the futile.
All the old possibilities—corrigendious, bone-headed and radiant—are here.

from *Jump Soul*

Jump Soul

. . . spirit like an aviary in one of the old zoos—
nets, gym-high ceiling—when an off-handed clap, scutter—
some disturbance—comes and the birds
fly wildly. No way to calm them down, no keeper's close attendance,
lights, jungle music, tame twittering of paddock avionics,

only the patternless mad fling of bodies and the engendered memory—
not even memory, only blood spat into the brain—
of vast green tracts and courtly practice, fig trees
filled with purple fruit, birdlings, cuties,
no goshawks in sight, the broad, banded, unbuckled sky
and coherent sunshine luffing calmly, not for them.

Who Knows If That Would Work

Repetitions might work, for example
                                        the bald Russian vacillator
showing up at the party beat to shit
         wearing a hospital bracelet stamped
                                                                        Unknown Unknown;
or my love's story
where they were never in the milk bar you like so much;
or the double set of figured curtains,
                                        rustling as if dawn's conclusive;
or backyard
       and frontyard;
or the river with its matching banks
                                                     still damp
from rain in which every drop
said the exact same thing—
                                                     like me
with my fixations and night sweats
rearing from the dust
and acclaim of dreams, my interest in you
       suspect, yet each day
              revivified, little white boat of love
rounding the bend toot toot.

Why We're Here

. . . the dramatic reading of my love letters
my secret thoughts in which
I danced with the dictator all night a fretful and uneasy
sort but lovable and now the country classics

are playing my old come-hithers
the sopping costume I wore
for years like a sodality, the pressurized capsule
I spent my summers in

taunting the losers, all these manufactured
houses of love, the crab-walk to the governor's palace,
have come back from the dead—or were never dead they say,
only sapped—the despised and

useless
were really my best friends
and the crapped-out have come to tell me
it's raining in dixie and the gross

taunts I overheard have been converted into well-run niceties
and what was the name of that boy
the fretful child barefoot in the pantry
I popped in the back of the head as I went by.

Shakespeare in the Villages

It's another dusty afternoon on Godzilla Street.
            The rattled little monarchs and their kin,
the blustery cartoons, what's obvious and about
to take over—something unusual, I guess—
    a stillness betided with grief,
                                        someone speaking
with a pal about ducats, ducats and wine,
all this, and the minute fractions
    of temperament,
            the little drawings tossed in the trash,
it's got to mean something,
like an adage,
the give-and-take of the fracas, the way one
    thing without comment replaces another, you saw it,
new people operating the jewelry store,
now it's a shop that sells hampers and buckets, interiors no one's lived in yet.

The Plot Is the One Thing We Know

Some record put together
of individual
    portions

the slick monkey paw leaves

    and arrested
    growth in the backlogged

pines somebody says *would you look at*

that
and you wonder what
                        pass by without
    finding out the little

appurtenances soft sensibilities
you employ

            to escape the brechtian
            possibilities
                        the empty city pools

they used for arenas

and now

    they're comfortably
                                    returned from
prison
the huge pads

    over the eyes the blank spaces
    between here

and the hinges—

    outside the world's

battered
and ready
for the fryer—

            you take
            a little hit

my father says
    from his grave
            and you go on

under the folds of the earth the caesars
sid and julius
constitutionalists

    the overly prepared

churning in the afterwash

    of whatever
    it was
    propelled all this.

Collected First Lines

I'm not saying I'm confused by the way a flock
of blackbirds makes me think
an organization's moving its headquarters,

but I wonder about the elusive silvery momentum
of certain fish, animals
avoiding sunlight, the way a river cracks

open into white, discursive signatures;

I'm not opposed to valuable heirlooms
found tucked in a sack of potatoes,
the cleric's garb and two-tone shoes
in the whore's back room;

I'm not surprised at wasted days,
whole seasons spent in the wrong house;

I've positioned myself near the suicide's regalia,
the sharpened blade, the pistol, the noose
(I like to poke these items with the toe of my boot);

I've taken the measure of certain lost causes,
resisted in a quiet way the release

of records that would shed an unhappy light on the case;

I've half deliberately lost my way,
exchanged pitiful glances, curried favor
with undeveloped bloodlines, dogged it;

I've compared notes with fools and found myself wanting;

I'm not claiming a special privilege,
I don't want my back pay;

I caught myself staring into a barrel
and was unable to confirm what I saw there;

as in the misplaced manifesto,
I'm sure there is meaning,
and I know it's sometimes more interesting
to stand in a road than to move along it,

though even this, said with such confidence
just a minute ago,

explains nothing.

Just a Note

fall picks at the sycamores

and the rain attempts to insert its ringless fingers into the padlocked
summer suitcases that when prized open

reveal in their vast bogs where the setbacks are stored,
the slackjawed corpses
that never learned the lingo, whole civilizations packed in the dead mouths

of those who mixed up what they valued
with a tinkling sound they heard as a child, who at odd times

remembered flowering dogwoods floating among pines
and a reticence they were unable to shake, even at the trials that stood in

for their lives, who found

the swimming pools shuttered
under brown canvas, burger stands closed, and the lifeguards fled to Florida.

Little Georgias

All these books I don't read anymore like the towns
I no longer go to, racked burgs
and hamletitos, gateways to loneliness—Bible readers
flipping pages to find the passage that reads
HEAVEN OPEN: FREE TO ALL, tiny grim children
sucking the heads of miniature dolls
as if stunned in sandy side streets
their parents like trees with the bark
stripped by lightning up one side, abjectly dying,
and those rainy afternoons in winter that stick in the mind
like something out of Dante
or Thorstein Veblen, the whole house damp,
the rain drilling into its one
hundred and fifth day, only Arnell Williams,
wrapped in a torn pineapple quilt,
trudging through the sand drifts on her way to the package store.

Used to Be More One-Eyed Men

. . . used to be more one-eyed men,
more crippled men and obscure backward men
half-crazy from teasing,
who did their personal business in an alley
and came up later with powdered sugar on their lips
asking questions
about lightning, used to be women
who scrubbed clothes with corncobs,
who stood amply foursquare, used to be men
without purpose continuing on, used to be women
turned into wraiths, and naked boys throwing rocks,
used to be a long way to the river, we'd ride the mules,
used to be a timeless sense to life,
used to be horrible occurrences just over the ridge,
women mutilating dead enemies, men
pissing in another man's eyes, used to be the grime
wouldn't come off, the waste was interminable,
used to be the jealous uncle
still alive, plotting revenge, used to be
less pavement, villages without sidewalks,
used to be a path through the fields to the lover's house,
used to be drunks and solitaries sleeping on the docks,
used to be elevated talk, phrasings like
varnished yachts turning in the canal, flowers in bunches
left on the porch, there were intricate performances,
felicities without justification or reason, used to be
a farmer fell in love with a town girl and never spoke of it,
not for forty years, and later, after he died,
you could ponder the corpse laid out on the bed,
and there was always some cousin rifling the boxes,
used to be a diary you came on with stilted confessions,

the love of a woman barely discernible in the bad writing
and choked-off feelings, used to be someone
would scarcely realize what this farmer had gone through,
someone almost not related who rocking on the porch later
recalled a phrase from the diaries,
something about what the farmer *saw,*
and understood he loved a woman,
used to be this was enough, a memory like this
passed down haphazardly from father to son, later
worked out in a story or a script, a grain of it alive
in the heart of one ambitious for fame
or simply peace, used to be you
could repeat this in your own life obscurely,
experience the tender insistence, the weird, crippled hope.

It Gets a Little Hazy

The years in Cuba are behind me now.
Little spotted dogs, like tiny archangels
followed me around. I smelled of salt
and palm oil. Given the nature

of belief, the effectiveness of the divine will,
unforgettable and strictly
for the birds, I could be said
to be out of touch. I read Aeschylus—

the diaries—*Othello on the Beach,*
and Peter Gunn. I gave my change
to private charities, something personal
I devised. Her lipstick

smelled like a clown's face. We practiced
tricks the Ringling Brothers taught her.
I supported small retainers,
converts and muralists struggling with

the dialect. We waked,
often at dawn, and lay
in the sheets cursing quietly. *I will*
particularize and dissuade, she said,

but it made no difference. I wore hats
of coconut frond and drove a Russian car.
My retreat from life
fit like a glove. Some nights

strange memories, passing for dreams,
of mud-caked shoes, cats
on the table eating scraps, and young men
caressing the faces of their superannuated lovers.

I shivered sometimes. I was on a long run
of quirky asides. *Take the monkey,* she said, *and go.*

Night Squishes the Sun Out Along the Treeline

I left out of there in a Pontiac I stole from one of my brothers and drove until I was too tired to go on. In a field in Virginia I rested under some oaks and watched a rolling flock of blackbirds devise another entrance point into the mystery of being. After a while I drove on to a little town where the mayor was hanging his laundry on a line beside the house. He said he knew me but this was not true. I gave him a sandwich and we sat on his front steps talking about the ruins of our lives. He harped on alignment and succulence, I spoke my piece about the universal buttering up going around. We sat there until the stars had wheeled around to face the other way. You could smell the asphalt plant across town. Time's rusty chains held us as we leaned back into our solitudes like children on a barge hauling them downriver to their worthless foster homes.

The River

I was supposed to fly down to see my brother,
but I got sidetracked by some girls
and was two days late. The place was shut up
and my brother was gone to the river to be
with the mangroves & knobby-headed egrets.
Down there the sun is so bright you can tell
that time will have no trouble with any of us.
I looked for a key to the house, but couldn't
find it and went to see a broker who tried to
sell me the patch of woods we played in as boys.
I didn't want the woods that were monstrous
and filled with demons and the vapors of rot.
He wanted me to drink with him but I wouldn't.
I have to find my brother, I said, and he laughed
and said, *You have no brother*, and I didn't
know what he meant, but I do now. I have
started for the river so many times, but some-
thing always comes up and I turn aside like
one who hears a band playing. Love is the key
to my brother's house, but he is gone to the river.

Whom Mothers Steer Their Children From

At eight what to wear was my big concern,
whether the jeans
with yellow cavalry stripe

crayoned into the seam, or my engineer
boots with ankle strap
and stainless steel rusting buckle,

or whether
to wear a hat
as the men did, soft snap-brims

that concealed
their faces from anyone spying above,
or a cap

with white letter J on it
for the local baseball Jays,
a set of farm team

weepers who never won a game.
Since I was four I'd
been a worrywart, nervous about

failure and edgy,
scared I would turn crazy and throw the cat
in the river

like Joe David Sims,
or slip matches into my pocket
to burn down

the Katy woods,
a tense boy
with motives he couldn't understand,

who in the gleaming dusk
watches across the paved road
as firemen

uncoil their grim hoses,
smiling calmly
to himself—hatted, in boots

and cavalry pants—as flames streak
up pine tree flanks
to catch the birds in their nests.

Spell

I see about half the spell life's put on me, maybe less.
A bird singing fully wild tunes in the pittosporum,
a creature so close, a regular, issuing its indecipherable bulletins,
reliable, compact, interposed between me
and the roar in my head; it's something to be grateful for.

I wake up thinking I'm nearly done and fear bites me like a dog.
Sun's already slipped in among the ruellia and the ficus,
I taste dust from old, rarely visited cities in my mouth.
Philosophies, kingdoms, swim through my eyes
like prison fields glimpsed from a passing pickup truck.

Red Cotton

My wife's in the kitchen melting plastic spoons,
I'm out back
coaxing the cat out of a mincemeat pie.
Symbolically in these matters we're connected—
like captains on distant windjammers,
one on fire,
the other signaling for a second helping.

I smell of pecans—a slightly sour
odor like rusted license plates.

Lately, I like to drive around town in the notary's car,
the world's smallest. He kept a snake
under the backseat, but the snake died.
The remains have a dusty old garbage smell,
and faintly, when I turn the corner, rattle.

I still don't know what kind of man I am.

I press my lips to red cotton,
red cotton panties, and sigh.

Delirious

In Miami
not a moment too soon
the hookers
who don't want to be alone yet
ask if I'd like a little morning massage
the sun's rising
like someone stepping from a barroom fight
the pace is killing
and just right like the sound of songbirds
as the clouds dissolve
everything's trying to keep a lid
on the terror
be good about the gaps
those bright bits broken off the fuselage
maybe they're new stars
like gods
from the other side of the world
throwing bodies in the air
catching fire
there's a list
we're always adding to
ours
and the one we're on

Taps in Key West

Up-tipped, half-stoved-in barrel crusted with white cochinas,
that's the island, calcific, glozed to a sheen, bobbing in the Gulf's backstream.

Proleptic, grazed by dawn, a lank breeze rouses in the mangroves
and stirs the herons into life. Day unrolls like a towel with all the states

painted on it, or a love letter composed in barbecue sauce, marked up
with stipulations and bughouse claims, handwriting like a kidnapper's,

IN CAPITALS, each word with a stupefied silence before and after.
This winter gamefish washed by thousands to the sidelines and the manatees

sank like adiposal gangsters shod in cement. Now spring's hacked itself
loose and the trees shoulder their gaudy epaulets. Birds like painted thumbs

nicker at the rooflines. The sun builds its coliseum. In the cemetery
dew daisies and yellow hawksbeard bristle, ready to repel armies of the dead.

Supposition

Lately I've throttled back, like a burglar
changing his face, one dab,
one touch of eye gloss, at a time.

I drive by the graveyard to visit Mother,

but she's still not there. I make sorties
to the mall, investigate a high-pitched whine,

buy milky-blue curtains and stop at the ocean
to see if they match. Sudsy swells
and oblates, the casual way a heron snaps up a fish,

the stink of sea grass, press against my knowledge of what's coming
like the din from a shift in government
in a country where we failed to beat the charges.

I sense the phantom musculature surrounding
old love affairs,
now warped and peeling like wooden tennis rackets. I entreat

the dusk with its genial
dispersals, its sun faded to a reference in the pittosporum.

Comely, not at all foreign,
dereliction presents the bill.

My soul, faded to jells and darns,

drapes like a thrift store shawl
across the shoulders of my ex-wife's old Pontiac.

Bus to Tuxtla

Sometimes you wait a while for the bus—
the bus to happiness
probably—just now passing the fried pie hutch
or crossing the stream like an old lady
carefully lifting her knees from the water—bus of transversal
and hopefulness—sometimes you wait all afternoon
and into the twilit hours, when, as time reverses slightly,
you feel the scarlet undergarments brush your cheek
as they go by, as the vastness disguised as a young girl passes,
sometimes, as the bus that is entering the outskirts of the ancient city
you've loved but never been at home in, bus with the face
of a tiger painted on the front, growling
to a stop at the marshy local park
where an old woman slowly growing used to being alone
waits quietly—sometimes, like a man of weary but unconquerable faith,
you wait all your life for the bus with its equipage of silver
rods and checked-cloth seats, its companionable
or fractious passengers, some growing weary now,
some broken beyond repair, others still hoping for an easement—
wizard or laundress—one for whom the door,
with an exculpatory gush, will open,
and as one ascending the last few steps into heaven
will rise, dreaming of a breeze lifting
slender curls of new vine in the old vineyard
that's gone now, and grasp the silver rod like the impossible means
into a paradise once hoped for on earth and nearly
found one afternoon among sequins and discarded undergarments
under a tamarind tree with a lover
who's dead and faded to haze and misremembered gestures—
and find a seat,

and just now, not long before the bus
reaches her stop,
disappears like the Mixotec kings into time.

Offhand

The heat creeps in like a ghost ship,
releasing its vaporous crew to overrun the town.
Something like this on Friday last. Shadows digging
a tunnel to freedom, the sun's constant shelling wearing
us down. I gather my old burgundy robe about me,
totter to the kitchen for a drink of ad hominem.
Bullace flowers drift through the garden
like souls on their way to the convenience store.
I'm older than I ever was, younger than
I'll ever be again. My luggage waits
on the porch, the sample cases I'm returning.
I didn't get that far into things, the murks
and rackets, but I liked the grassy
salients I sometimes stood on gazing at the water.

from *Demo*

Here, Dog

You say dogs
prefer the smell of the people they love
    and say everyone, even whole groups, according
to what they eat
and how they are arranged, emit a typical smell
    their dogs can recognize, and the way they look contributes to this
and how they move like ponies
crashing through bamboo
    or crushed souls fleeing midnight rooms, and rarely do dogs
if ever get mixed up
about this,
    they're always on the lookout as night
enters the ancient streets
without signs or balustrades wound
    with roses, and you say the dogs are here, standing stiff-legged
by the hedge or writhing in happiness,
and you, sweating,
    or stinking of an angry lover's perfume, are recognizable
and taken in, a wanderer
troubled or excised from the rolls,
    resentful, or nervous about money, the dog has put you
under his wing
and hurries you into the familiar estancia
with a love that can't be lost
    or beaten out of him as it has been lost and beaten out of you.

This Water Tastes of Iron

My tattoos tell love's story in miniature, which I prefer.
My dips in style, the picture I painted on a pool cover,
express a reckless calm, unsubstantiated but plush.
I pray to the ticking sound I hear at night. Breezes,
shaped in Africa, remind me of friends
buried in the sea. For years I lived in a home for the blind,
working the semaphore. My over-obvious
rectitude bought only time. Let's drain
the dark, she said, from every room. The mottos
on the radio scratch lately at my door, unverifiable
and hilarious. The past sinks like a body in a well.
I read the Bible for the stakeouts and descriptions of terrain.

Why Harp on It

In the stillness of dawn when the air hangs back and you plunge your hand
into the bottomless dark of a jasmine
bush when roosters crack the day open under a slurry sky and you've
forgotten why you're awake
and don't know why you're thinking of the time you gave the go ahead
for your mother's shock treatments and she came out
blank and ironical unable to squeeze orange juice and you poured her a drink
and she said Thank you I am very tired
and you were moving to Sioux City and didn't have time to say good-bye
and for a couple of years lived in a motel
and ate Chinese-Mex and supported a young car hop who needed
the money for her rattled
child and you'd wake at dawn with your deepest bones
aching like you'd gotten old before your time and there was no way
to be sure of anything and red gazelles
atlas bears heath hens blue walleyes thicktail chubs
sea minks dire wolves catahoula
salamanders and xerces blue butterflies were already gone from the earth.

Crostatas

in rome I got down among the weeds and tiny perfumed
flowers like eyeballs dabbed in blood and the big ruins
said do it my way pal while starlings
kept offering show biz solutions and well the vatican
pursued its interests the palm trees like singular affidavits
the wind succinct and the mountains painted blue
just before dawn accelerated at the last point
of departure before the big illuminated structures
dug up from the basement got going and I ate crostatas
for breakfast and on the terrace chatted
with the clay-faced old man next door and said I was
after a woman who'd left me years ago and he said lord aren't we all.

This Right Here

In restricted access, in lockdowns,
with a price on the goods, the particulars
    shrouded, wearing trash cans for boots, the spring,
that won't testify, the cunning
like a worm in the guts of its own stupidity, braced against the seawall,
the spring, and why would I say this, or better,
let me tell you about the wildwood, that slumped masterpiece
    tick infested teeming with bugs,
the stinking ocean sloshing onto the rusticated shore,
you notice this in springtime like a calculation
continually misfiring, like a scrap of paper left on the table
explaining the shootout, the dishonor at dawn,
    and something bangs against me, I am overmatched
by a morning with rain, by the compressors
the catafalques groaning, you say it's springtime
and the birds, troubled with psychosis,
their wings stained with creosote, press northward,
    compelled by a remarkable idiocy, uninvented,
hauling their bodies through the standard acidity
and friendlessness into dune shadows
like the breath of satire, it's spingtime
and runners are expected from the gravediggers
    with an appeal for more shovels, and the vines
crawl like murdered drunks
crawling in the dreams of their children, fiddling with the locks.

Samsara

The ocean, uncomfortable with itself, bangs and slurs,
mixing flavors, holding its own against infinity, scarred with ice. I rummage
in the window planter, arrange purslane and sundew to catch
the fairskinned day's best looks; the sun, winter's ear bob, hangs in a blue left to fade.

I'm going home, sings the celebrated pianist downstairs, a man of Africa,
traveled ages to sit before the #2 Concerto in A Minor. In my dream, cabbage roses
offered by my former wife, who stood wrapped in a red Navajo blanket
by the doorway of an old hogan on the rez, shone. She's gone now,

into the far lands of chaos; sun-shaped molecules, scent of sweet bay,
figurations of reordered atoms I'll never recognize without a guide, all that's left.
These dreams let me know we're still together,
dancing before headlamps on the beach, or converting

our savings bonds to cash for a run to Old Mexico. The sun swings along,
carrying an old silver pocketbook—or that's the moon,
jaunty, not so pushy really, only too happy to forget the night. Plum flowers
and the first pear blossoms, all the white concatenations gather

at the bottom of the yard. The wind picks up speed,
remembering its days in Paris, in Ihpetonga and Tobruk. Conversions
at this latitude are frequent, but rarely sustained; the old ways
were more comfortable, the pies and Franco-American customs, dollops

of pure cane syrup on biscuits, the rye grass streaked by invisible hand,
still pretty irresistible. I've caught up lately on everything
but time. An old leak, faintly corrosive, smelling of
uncleaned butter churns, whistles as it goes by, not minding much of anything.

Lacquered Dead

Balled-up clouds above the graveyard dab the shine off stars.
The dead fume up, spurious and superior, exchanging
love's gaudy reasons for a sub-section replacement
of elementary particles. Like you I'm a dying tribe. What I know
shines a moment—like leaves the cat licks—then returns to its place in line.
Get ready, the prophet says, but overlooks the dream-stalked,
the solitaries rowing the Straits of San Juan, loose flubbers
out walking the pinched streets of Fez. A taw-eyed woman on the edge
of madness leans from an upper story, catching all of space in one goggled glance.
Queer blue sky smeared with zinc. Each of us bent into one of the shapes
God makes. Fudged by will. Foot bones, casters, melon rinds—
emptiness, the future—wash in the runoff. Living's the least of it.

(Adirondack)

Something's falling in increments of banging and slight popping, klunks,
and then little
chittering rolls,
the roof I mean is being hit by objects
nuts, fruits
of the season: this miserable natural world
hurls these things . . . and then there're the wolf howls
or coyotes
as they call
them here and the barks and snuffles of so-called bears
and yesterday I saw a small tub-bottomed bishop
crossing the road on all fours—porcupine,
they said—and crows
strut
and there are these mincing deer so theatrically bold
and turkeys like drab bloated chickens
and tiny
bronze frogs
singing in my shoes
and last night as in the car I huddled over a radio broadcast
the stars lit up
in uncanny
formations: bright pegs
pictures of my tormentors and ex-wives . . . seemed to hang from:
and I showed them the frogs: shiny as coins of the caesars.

Volto

A spacial infirmity, what's closed-up like a child in a closet,
calls too softly to be heard. Like the little stream
with the broken back, that behind the barn collects
the bitter run-off. A specialized sky foretells the fall
of humankind. Clouds like saggy diasporas.
The fields flex their big muscles, getting ready for the stare-down
with the stars. It's winter, then summer comes
perfumed with toiletries. Raspberries bend quadrate
branches, the fruit like children about to swing into eternity.
I'm limited, she says, *but not alarmed, and ineffectively violent.*
Sometimes we block love like dump trucks on strike at the kiln.
The closed-off future taps at the window. It's the echo
that's scary. Suffering completes its tax return,
listing no dependents. The papered-over bits have shifted in the night.
Grim looks grimness in the eye. The dead taste of salt.
At the site tiny storms rage among the balled-up dresses.
Someone's heart's split open and used for a mask.
Sounds like love, says the mayor, *but then to me everything does.*

Wilderness

rain like drops of cold lead—
it's hard in this city to keep a grip on the natural world
poking its snout through the wovenwire fence on 7th
or while ordering fried chicken to go on Ave C
where once the carts like tiny sailing ships brought
alarm clocks and unblessed remnants the linden leaves
and locust leaves like green insertions blow
down 5th to meet the stiff leaves of bur oaks
and elm leaves like slender jimmies for all the locks
of memory on 8th—the remains of a garden
or lost civilization rise to a grassy mound where
children veer into fantasy and only bits of spotless sky
torn from a secret book appear above the lost and broken.

From Heine

Wo wird einst des Wandermüden . . .

Where will I lie in the bye and bye
where will I lie?
In the fresh snow under northern lights
permafrosted in a stony field?
In a desert hole
of mixed borax and sandstone dust?
With a few dozen others tossed
in a pit after a friendly fire massacree?
Or slumped untended
on a weary slog from one unsuitable
home to the next
ex-animate and overlooked?
Anyhow, the whole policky skittish harangue
of comets and skirly
planet types space dust and infinite
jitters will surround me, lamps of a looted paradise.

One Spell

Now these redbirds,
cowbirds, flickers making
noise in the boxwoods, jasmine
trellis, thrushes and vireos
clambering in the straw, poking
out the eyes of children,
and bugs, waxwings, catbirds in
wax myrtle bushes, yaupons,
heart-wing sorrel plants in
cutover fields, warbler and oven
bird saying *teach-er, teach-er,*
nobody showing up for months,
mother drunk under the vines,
redstart and bobolink, lover
of hayfields and grasslands,
oriole hardly ever away
from the nest, mass migrations
of blackbirds and other seed eaters,
songbirds, all gone from here.

The Casing

For years I sat in bars lying about everything,
concealing my limp, offering vinyl
suitcases for sale and proposing to women
who'd overlooked themselves. I gave away

folding tables and threatened
species like lopsided turtles and misused
harness bulls. I wasn't as speedy as I claimed to be
or as galled by those without

a purpose in life. I sold three-day
vacations to resorts that existed
only in my mind. I liked to watch the breeze
take leafy boughs in hand.

The limits to man's ability
to reach the stars were no problem for me.
I sank my nose in foreign papers
looking for tiny lots I might build

my dream house on. I said I owned
hotels and racks for smoking arctic char.
I claimed to notice something burning
in the kitchen. A leaf seemed at times to urge

a change in plans. Probably the winds
were coming from the other quadrant. I gave away
my watch and told the time by the degradation
of building materials. I spelled the stuporized.

The sun, an old friend, eased
onto the brickyard wall. I sensed an era
drawing to a close. Something told me,
so I said, to gather my things. Smoothed-

over ideas, frets, a capacity for change
unremarked by others, a boarding house
menu I used for a text, my bindle, palpebral musings,
a burial suit of lights

and a jar of brandied apricots—all these
I said I'd send a van back for and never did.

No Nonsense

split off for a sec
I thought I might say something
truthful
but couldn't come up with it
and lingered in the rosy twilight
unpacking an old suitcase
I found under the stairs

sometimes I stay as still
as possible and tell myself
a limitless vista's
opening up when it's not

the rain pounded madly on the roof

afterwards we
sat on the porch shelling
peas and quoting scripture

the birds in the melaleuca trees
seemed tired

the sky
reopened like a grocery store
on a desert road

I came
away from myself
unstuck

and a sort of translucent
orderliness
like a small herd of gazelles
entered my mind

Ithika

private disputes in the sweet apple
trees and a certitude

attested to by loquats and the hard-shell baptist
spiders

collecting rents

the way you look at me after you knock me
silly with kisses

and what's up with the elementals I say
the dog

lurks in the cabana like Ulysses
shadowing his old lady

the calculations
    fixing the tide

and *the inexpressible* surrounding the fort
these particulars

left over
when we boiled the affidavits

add up
to the spitting image

of true north
she says

covering her left eye with the hand
holding the deed

to the trailer
and a crushed floral tribute

and suppose—she says—
my typical effervescence was replaced

by an obscurity
heretofore unmentioned in the ranks

and the mock
voyage

turned out
to be the voyage.

Backseat in Kinshasa

a crisis averted in gulfport pops up again in forest hills
or someone's talking about a job bucking timber or after a cold
lobster supper on the cape its fabricator forgets the singular phrase
that explains everything and then you're revoking
yesterday's permit or tailing a cheat across lower manhattan
or you've just changed the name of your dreamboat and it's time
for your pills or it's time for a check-in with the vastness
and the preacher is crying over the dappled gray running last
in the fourth at pimlico and the bomb removal squad is just leaving
your apartment or you are unable to drop the loose talk outside
filene's basement or spring is nowhere near this town
and the operators all reach home at the same time and you understand
everything means something else and weren't told that cabbage roses
went out of style or the proceeds from the caper long ago were lost

No Claim

A tense obligato, the light comes up out of a shallow grave.
It was only resting. Sulphur butterflies, taking a holiday
in the garden, one in shades of yellow and orange, the other
the same plus chestnut spots, drift above
white-faced mallows, giving a sense of softness, richness
to the situation, paralleling the stinks and murder
poking up everywhere, each an elaboration of presence, minus
idea and will, the soul, we think, something like this,
gliding through the somatological world, airy, when maybe it's not,
maybe just an overweight bumbler, clumsy sporting-goods salesman
of the spirit, slumped by the road in a used Eldorado with
the window down, sweating in the dog-day heat, one we pass
irritably, exhumaceously by, as we hurry to the rendezvous.

Issues with a Right-Hand Turn

Sometimes I'm issued a new head
and the old one drops
off and then I see the new one isn't new
it's a used
head, sometimes a bit moldy
or flushed
with rage, this head
filled with notes on what is wrong with the world
or carrying a list
of expendables or groceries
a head that remembers sunset casting
a golden shine
into the wheat
or the painting of a pig on a dinner plate,
or once I got
a head filled with memories
of snowy nights
when she dared me to love her, but I couldn't
speak the part
and had to set this head down
beside the road
and go on for the rest of that episode
headless, heedless,
one you couldn't hang for his crimes
if you wanted to.

This Far'll Do

the coast along here smells
like a rusty washing
machine still
in use. the sudsy
clouds are in on this. the sharks and flounders
know what's going on.
old plaques and busted dance floors
teeter among brushy
trash. discolored boilers filled with
bullet holes rest
like blue whales in the spit-
colored sand.
you can't walk ten feet
without
having to crawl over something.
skate eggs
shrivel in gray
sunlight. slithers of sea lettuce rot.
the meaning
of the world is in plain sight.
crabs line up
to turn themselves in. three hots
and a cot would do fine.
redfish belch
and puke up supper. the fix
is in—everybody
knows this.
we're beyond catastrophe
says the cod.
you could go on forever, but why bother.

Stroke

In the latest web of branches,
cuddled and
softened by a clandestine wind, before a sky clotted
and gauged and calling home to mama
who's dead, the taste of oranges in your mouth,
a moment when you stand
helpless before all you know about
yourself, a soft voice speaks. *Shake that back end, buddy.*
Meanwhile the tiny propellers and antique
aircraft turn. You smell the bony
dust in
the prairie grass. Sometimes your favorite
color changes
to aqua. *Everything's*
collapsible, the guy next to you on the subway
platform says. You're up
for the Simple Simon
part, a precision
unknown in your circle. Galvanized
washtubs stacked
in front of the funeral home. *Parts,* a woman sez.
A child at the curb works out his route
to fortune.
The cities at the corners of the map
are beginning to droop.
We remember how funny that was
the first time.

Bolt Upright

home from work my father
would throw himself face down writhing
on the old couch as if he was smothering a fire
his body raw
from the chemicals at the plant
his wrists revealing the cords he was stretched by
that pulled him into
jaundiced shapes
and left him spinning in fumes
the disaster of his life that he endured
without mentioning
it even to my mother who
fixed elaborate suppers from a book she found
at the library
and never returned
at the table they would hunch shamefaced
over their food
like the early primates
who knew nothing of the world
outside the woods
no sense of broadway or of rooms filled
with paintings scattering the beauty of life before them
not even a religion
or a hope only us children
they lifted their battered heads
and stared at as if
we were creatures just called back from the dead
that they did not remember.

Belfast

I woke up still trying to understand things
and something about the moist smells of early morning
the collapsible flowers
pretending everything's all right
really got to me as if I was a monk standing in a dry river bed
trying to recall what the world was like
before he left it, and I drove to the supermarket
and got a bucket of chicken and thought about Rachel
who's probably driving home from work now
in Belfast, maybe talking as she drives to the handsome detective
she's dating, and sometimes I think of lakes, clear and taut
after the wind dies, of how voices travel far over them
unhindered at dusk no matter what you are saying.

Counting on My Fingers

snow day for the soul she says
and pulls out her list of plants that thrive in winter
hemlock pines firs
shimmying in sunlight evergreen
live oaks ilex
laurel and camellias boxwood holly
the stiff drapes
of mahonia represented
as colorful on snowy days when trains
pant lonely on
suburban tracks and old men
press their faces
against loved ones like representatives
of a culture
that could kill you easily juniper
and daphne she says aucuba the streaked stiff leaves
of moonshadow
hemlock cedar on the path
down to the beach where a girl was murdered
ceanothus hoarding blue
puffballs pyracantha
thorn putting out the eye of a child
everywhere you
look something bearing down arbutus
bottlebrush rhododendron
once in the mountains viburnum we slept under
she says and I remember that time
like a rent in my heart

Minor Fabrications

sometimes I wish
I was a professional scooter or braiser or concrete analyzer
of fragmented evenings
in the moonlight, a caster of lines
maybe
sailer of paper plates
poker of holes
or one whose hands have massaged a heart
or two
calling come on, baby, give,
or something
like that. you can walk around on this earth
carrying a watermelon
or a proviso
detailing the mysteries of the cosmos,
but it's best
to have some professional
experience on your record, a slip
of paper
that says so, and memories
like the taste
of muscadines and mashed potato
sandwiches late at night
in a diner off the highway,
where just now
the cook lies slumped at the coatrack
shot through the heart
by love. nobody wants to be left out
or controlled by vacuous
malingerers
or managers of rerun houses where the stars

try to prepare us
for the worst. even at dam sites
and trails
in reticulated woods after dark
someone is calling for a pro. let us
pick up our instruments
and go. with only a little training
it could be you,
maybe me, handling the stroke, the delve.

Unattainable Goodness

What is it I belong to and find like crushed mint on my shoes,
the stepped rocks presented like a change of heart

that speaks to me as if we are of the same brotherhood,
the casual significance of a bird passing over this field, the way the painter,

with a flick of the brush, made me stop to think first of my father,
then of dying, and how then I was a small boy again,

afraid to make a mistake and alert all the time like the French in Indochina
—what is it I belong to like a residual effect, a remark

dropped handily into the conversation to prove love still exists,
the way—as we went on—the congressman couldn't come up

with an example (that satisfied us) of the soul on lend-lease,
or, in the high valley, how we liked to stay up late, reading the old books

Mother used to keep in the kitchen, until finally Father would come out,
a look in his eyes of a wintering sadness, and tell us to go to bed.

One

Some you approach through the woods carrying cakes
Some you sneak up on as if they are orphans
    bandaging the wings of birds
Some you refer to as inconspicuous even though you see them everywhere
Some you place inside your hat and walk around with all day
    as if you are balancing an egg on your head
Some you discover living in the Denver Y
Some you convert to a useless piece of dialogue
Some you fitfully oppose
Some you apply to meekly explaining yourself
    in freakish and ill-favored French
Some you travel to far countries with
Some you misplace
Some you pick the under feathers off of and murmur to fondly
Some you obviously compare to a vanished wilderness
Some you watch dwindle in the rear view mirror
Some you place on the windowsill
Some you embrace without passion
Some you speak to in barrooms and art galleries
    referring to yourself as fraudulent and unfathomable
Some you dispense with lightly
Some you divert into other professions
Some you understand as disguised by moonlight
Some you prepare for a better life
Some you poke
Some you unnerve while dreaming of hotels by the sea
Some you righteously anger
Some you offer pastries to
    and lose sight of frequently
Some you heckle and deride
Some you take casually to your bosom

Some you compare to mice living in granaries
Some you watch from the corner of your eye
Some you badger and push to great acts
Some you dispense with
Some you teach a short solo
Some you love
Some you don't know what to do with
Some you clearly can't speak to without blushing
Some you disturb
Some you compare to a short selection of musical numbers
Some you never get over

The Players

I get away among the other players
and practice my style which
includes a section
of close-packed
    moans and a sudden electrified turn
you might not
expect
    if you've never seen it before plus
a look of resolution
that dissolves so quickly
you might think it was
never there
    in the first place. there's a happiness
too you can see
through like a clear plastic
bag
filled with rainwater.
all the others are busy
practicing as well
    and this is one of the good parts.
I watch
and pick up a few pointers
and baldly
universal
techniques that
are a hit everywhere
and I get after them. and you
    too, I say to myself, you too are a hit.

Picture of the Situation

You don't call it pain
you call it daylight
or the rough bark of some oak tree
or the rocks like broken steps at the edge of the woods
but it's not pain
it's not even sadness or anything
you'd set aside or comment on in the diary
you compulsively keep.
Fierce words break through arguments
you get into out in the driveway.
You could set the house
on fire and stand there in the yard still arguing
about how you failed to love her
properly and the fire wouldn't affect you.
Now it's all back in the shed, the
hopes and fabulous way of putting things,
some shed you keep a lock on.
You stand out in the yard
picking the pine sap off the car hood waiting for her
to finish whatever she's
doing inside the house. You light a cigarette
and look at the match
and then you stand there with your head
thrown back. Whatever's pressed up against you
presses so hard breath can't get out. You can't even scream.

By Mechanical Means

Splintery, spring pretends
to stall. Crafted, succinct,
bog hemp & new wild
olive tremble

and appear indistinguishable
from sandspur
and Spanish dagger. Flat
fingers of rain, the care taken

before we set out for supper,
your brother standing a long time gazing
across the pasture
coming up in white clover, a sense

of opportunity missed, swung round
again. The Redeemer, in the body
of a truck gardener, ambles by on his way to the john.
Antinomian heresies

shade toward the barn. Cypresses
shaky in the woods, the proposals of winged
sumac and maidencane taken in stride,
soft landings for briar and crotalaria

bloom. The tiniest is taken
care of. Conventions appraised
and disputes settled. Cow oak and dogwood
seem to push back, extrude

calculated systems of foamy white.
Rambler time. The earnestness
of those who made it through winter
to this spot,

the usual phraseology
and cumbersome mechanics, a child
confessing a childish
crime, a gift carelessly given,

taken back. What's
worked through or failed at
or lost reaches the edge of the barrow
where sorrel

and inkberry thrive, where we loiter,
hunchbacks and enfeebled moralists,
palsied, convulsive, marooned
in this life, willing to talk about it now.

ACKNOWLEDGMENTS

To my editor, Jill Bialosky, and her hardworking staff at Norton, my deepest thanks for ushering this collection into the world. And many thanks to the editors and staff of the magazines in which many of these poems first appeared.

INDEX OF TITLES AND FIRST LINES